STRAIGHT ROAD
TO EXCEL 2013/2016
PIVOT
TABLES

SAM AKRASI

To order additional copies of this book, contact:
Xlibris
1-800-455-039
www.xlibris.com.au
Orders@Xlibris.com.au

DOWNLOADS

This book comes with practice exercises. To perform these exercises, you will need to download the Excel workbooks. These workbook files are available for download from the author's website at www.grandtotals. com.au or contact info@grandtotals.com.au. You can also download these files from the publisher's website at: www.samakrasisbooks.com.

WHAT YOU NEED TO USE THIS BOOK

You need a computer running a version of the Windows operating system, preferably Windows 10 or later. You also need Microsoft Excel 2013 or later. You can use any edition of Excel 2013/2016, but to get the full benefit of the book including the chapters on Power Pivot Data Models, you will need the PowerPivot add-in which ships with the Professional Plus edition of Excel.

For the single topic on OLAP you need SQL Server 2012 or higher installed on your computer and the Analysis Services instance on the server. For the same chapter, you need to download the AdventureWorks2014 sample database.

Table of Contents

DOWNLOADS iii

WHAT YOU NEED TO USE THIS BOOK iii

1. Beginning the Pivot Table Journey 1

    1.1. The Parts of a Pivot Table 1

        1.1.1.   Values Area 1

        1.1.2.   Rows Area 1

        1.1.3.   Columns Area 2

        1.1.4.   Filters Area 2

2. A Look At A Simple Pivot Table 3

    2.1. Shaping the Data 3

        2.1.1.   Data Must Be Tabular 3

        2.1.2.   Do Not Store data in Section Headings 4

        2.1.3.   Avoid Repeating Groups as Columns 4

        2.1.4.   Make Your Data Source Compact (No Gaps) 5

        2.1.5.   Apply Appropriate Type Formatting 5

        2.1.6.   Summary of Good Source Data Design 5

                EXERCISE 2a: 5

    2.2. Creating Your First Pivot Table 7

        2.2.1. Adding Fields to the Report 8

        2.2.2. Adding Layers to a Pivot Table Report 9

        2.2.3. Move Data Around 9

        2.2.4. Creating a Report Filter 10

2.3.   PivotTable Templates 11

2.4.   Slicers, What Are They? 12

   2.4.1. Creating a Standard Slicer 12

      Exercise 2a: 13

   2.4.2. Slicer Can Use Dates 14

      Exercise 2b: 16

2.5. Refreshing the Pivot Table Report 16

   2.5.1. When the Existing Data Source Changes 16

   2.5.2. When Rows and Columns EXPAND and Shrink 16

2.6.   A Look at the New Pivot Table Tools 17

   2.6.1. Suspending Updates 17

   2.6.2. Clear the Pivot Table Report 18

   2.6.3. Relocating the Pivot table 19

3. Customizing Your Pivot Table Report 20

3.1. Enhancing the Pivot Table Report 20

   3.1.1. Using the Table Style Features 20

   3.1.2. Formatting Numbers 21

   3.1.3. Replacing Blank Values with Zeros 23

   3.1.4. Changing a Field Name 24

3.2.   Making Changes to Report Layout 24

   3.2.1. Using the Compact Layout 25

   3.2.2. Using the Outline Form Layout 26

   3.2.3. Using the Tabular Layout 27

   3.2.4. Blank Lines, Grand Totals, and Other Settings 27

3.3. Enhance Your Report with Styles and Themes 28

   3.3.1. Creating Custom Styles 28

      Exercise 3A: Creating and Applying Custom Style 30

3.4. Applying Different Aggregation Functions 31

3.5. Displaying and Suppressing Subtotals 31

    3.5.1.   Remove Subtotals 32

    3.5.2.   Multiple Subtotals for A Single Field 33

3.6.   Using Different Calculation for Value Fields 33

    3.6.1.   Showing percentage of Total 34

    3.6.2.   Using %Of to Compare One Line to Another Line 34

    3.6.3.   Showing Ranks 34

        Exercise 3b: 34

4. Grouping, Sorting, and Filtering Pivot Data 37

4.1. Grouping Pivot Fields 37

    4.1.1.   Grouping Date Fields 37

    4.1.2.   Grouping Date Fields by Week 39

    4.1.3.   Ungrouping Your Data 40

        Exercise 4a: 40

4.2.   The PivotTable Fields List 43

    4.2.1.   Using the Areas Section Drop-Downs 44

4.3.   Sorting in a Pivot table 44

    4.3.1.   Using a Manual Sort Sequence 44

4.4.   A Look at Pivot Table Filters 45

4.5. Using Filters for Row and Column Fields 46

    4.5.1.   Filtering Using the Check Boxes 46

    4.5.2.   Filtering Using the Search Box 46

    4.5.3.   Filtering Using the Label Filters 47

    4.5.4.   Value Column Can Filtering Label Columns 48

    4.5.5.   Creating a Top-Five Report Using the Top 10 Filters 49

    4.5.6.   Filtering Using the Date Filters in the Label Drop-Down 50

4.6. Filtering Using the Filters Area 51

    4.6.1. Choosing One Item from a Filter 51

    4.6.2. Choosing Multiple Items from a Report Filter.........................51

    4.6.3. Distributing a Pivot Table Report for Each Item in a Filter........52

4.7. Filtering Using Slicers and Timelines...53

    4.7.1. Filtering by Date 55

5. Extend Columns and Rows with Calculations 57

5.1. Calculated Fields and Calculated Items 57

5.2. Creating a Calculated Field..58

    Exercises 5a: 59

5.3. Creating a Calculated Item...61

5.4. Calculations Live by Rules..65

    5.4.1. Using Cell References and Named Ranges 65

    5.4.2. Using Worksheet Functions..65

    5.4.3. Using Constants...65

    5.4.4. Referencing Totals and SubTotals 65

    5.4.5. Rules For Calculated Fields 65

    Exercise 5a:..66

    5.4.6. Rules For Calculated Items..67

5.5. Managing and Maintaining Pivot Table Calculations 67

    5.5.1. Editing and Deleting Pivot Table Calculations 67

    5.5.2. Documenting Formulas 68

6. Using Pivot Charts and Other Visualizations 69

6.1. Creating Your First Pivot Chart...69

6.2. Things to Know About Charts..71

    6.2.1. Pivot Table And Pivot Charts Work Together...........................71

    6.2.2. Placement of Data Field in Pivot Table 71

Exercise 6a: 72

6.2.3. Pivot Charts Can Evolve 75

6.2.3.1 Method 1: Turn Pivot table into Hard Values 75

6.2.3.2 Method 2: Delete the Underlying Pivot Table 75

6.2.3.3 Method 3: Distribute the Picture of the Pivot Chart 75

6.2.4. Conditional Formatting Can Apply to Pivot Tables Too................................. 75

6.2.5. Creating Custom Conditional Formatting Rules 77

7. Using Different Data Sources with Pivot Tables.. 81

7.1. Using Multiple Consolidation Ranges 81

7.2. Using the Internal Data Model... 86

7.2.1. Beginning Data Model... 86

7.2.2. Creating Relationships in the Data Model.. 90

7.2.3. Adding a New Table to the Data Model 91

7.2.4. Removing a table from the Data Model.. 92

7.2.5. Create New Pivot Table From Your Data Model 92

7.3. Building a Pivot Table Using External Data Sources.................................... 93

7.3.1. Building a Pivot table with Microsoft Access Data 94

7.3.2. Building a Pivot table with SQL Server Data.. 95

8. Introducing PowerPivot 99

8.1. Joining Multiple Tables Using the Data Model From Excel 2013/2016...................... 99

8.1.1. Preparing Data for Use in the Data Model 99

8.1.2. Adding the First Table to the Data Model 99

8.1.3. Adding the Lookup table and defining relationship 100

8.2. Creating a New Pivot Table from an Existing Data Model 102

8.3. Getting a Distinct Count 103

8.4. PowerPivot Add-In from Excel 2013 and Excel 2016 Professional Plus.................. 104

8.5. Using Text File Data Source... 104

Exercise: 106

8.6.   Add Excel Data by Copying and Pasting 106

8.7. Add Excel Data by Linking 107

8.8.   Define Relationships 108

8.9. Add Calculated Columns Using DAX 108

8.10. Build a Pivot table in the Data Model 109

8.11. Using the RELATED Function 110

8.12. Using a Calendar Table to Enable Time Intelligence Functions 111

    8.12.1. Adding the Data to PowerPivot and Formatting It 111

    8.12.2. Specifying Sorting Columns 112

    8.12.3. Create PivotTable From the Data Model 113

8.13. PowerPivot Time Intelligence 113

9. Creating Dashboards with Power View 116

9.1. Preparing Your Data for Power View 116

9.2.   Creating Power View Dashboard 118

9.3. Convert the Table to Chart 119

9.4. Add Drill-Down to a Chart 121

9.5. Beginning a New Element 122

9.6. Filtering Elements with Charts 122

9.7. Adding a Real Slicer 122

9.8. Changing the Calculation 123

10. Using OLAP Data For Data Model 124

10.1. Connecting to an OLAP Cube 125

10.2. Understanding the Structure of an OLAP Cube 128

    10.2.1. Performing What-If Analysis with OLAP data 129

1. BEGINNING THE PIVOT TABLE JOURNEY

A pivot table enables you to create an interactive view of your data set, called a *pivot table report*. With a pivot table report, you can categorize data into groups, summarize large amounts of data into meaningful information, and perform a variety of calculations quickly and easily. But the real power of a pivot table report is that you can interactively drag and drop fields within your report, dynamically changing your perspective and recalculating totals to fit your current view.

1.1 THE PARTS OF A PIVOT TABLE

A pivot table is composed of four areas. The data you place in these areas defines both the utility and appearance of the pivot table. These four areas are:

1.1.1 VALUES AREA

The **Values Area** is shown in Figure 1.1. It is a large rectangular area below and to the right of the headings. In Figure 1.1, the values area contains a sum of the revenue field. The Value area is the area that calculates. You must place at least one field in this area.

| Producer | (All) | | | | | | | ← Filter | | FIGURE 1.1 |

Sum of Revenue	Column Labels						
Row Labels	January	February	March	April	Mar	Apr	Grand Total
Cashew	$0	$139,589,791	$0	$0	$0	$0	$139,589,791
Cocoa	$99,222,408	$0	$0	$0	$0	$0	$99,222,408
Groundnuts	$0	$0	$0	$0	$0	$200,312,288	$200,312,288
Millet	$0	$0	$162,184,631	$0	$0	$0	$162,184,631
Shea Butter	$0	$0	$0	$0	$177,562,883	$0	$177,562,883
Soghum	$0	$0	$0	$251,166,342	$0	$0	$251,166,342
Grand Total	$99,222,408	$139,589,791	$162,184,631	$251,166,342	$177,562,883	$200,312,288	$1,030,038,343

Rows ↑   Values ↑

The data field you drop here are those you want to measure or calculate. The value area might, for example, include **Sum of Tonnage**, **Count of Units**, and **Average of Price**. It is also possible to have the same field dropped in the value area more than once, but with different calculations, such as **Minimum of Price**, **Average Price**, and **Maximum of Price,** in the same report.

1.1.2 ROWS AREA

The *Rows Area* shown, in Figure 1.1, is composed of the headings that go down the left side of the pivot table. Excel automatically displays the unique values from that field down the rows of the left side of the pivot table. The Rows area typically has at least one field, although it is possible to have no fields. The types of data fields you should drop here include those you want to group and categorize – for example, **Products**, **Names**, and **Locations.**

1.1.3 COLUMNS AREA

The *Columns Area* is composed of headings that stretch across the top columns in the pivot table. In figure 1.1, the month field is in the Column area. The column area is ideal to show trending over time, such as **Months, Periods, and Years**

1.1.4 FILTERS AREA

The *Filters area* is an optional set of one or more drop-downs at the top of the pivot table. In Figure 1.1, the filters area contains the **Producer** field, and the pivot table is set to show all producers. Dropping fields into the Filters area would enable you to filter the data items using that fields. The types of data fields you would drop here include those you want to isolate and focus on – for example, **Region, Line of Business**, and **Employees**.

2. A LOOK AT A SIMPLE PIVOT TABLE

Having familiarized yourself with the anatomy of a pivot table, let us turn your attention to how you should design your data to make it pivot table compatible

2.1 SHAPING THE DATA

The basic rule for preparing your data for pivot table reporting is that the data source must have column headings which are labels in the first row describing the information in each column

2.1.1 DATA MUST BE TABULAR

The ideal layout for the source data for a pivot table is a tabular layout, where the data is compact with no empty rows or columns. Every column has a heading. Every field has a value in every row. Columns do not contain repeating groups of data. So instead of having:

JanSales	FebSales	MarSales
5500	2340	7000

You should have:

Month	Sales
Jan	5500
Feb	2340
Mar	7000

Figure 2.1 shows an example of a properly structured data for a pivot table. There are headings for each column. Notice that the City, Dealer, and Model columns have repeated values such as **ABC Dealers**, these repetitions are necessary to allow the table to be used for a pivot table report. Exercise 1 demonstrates this principle. Month data is organized down the page instead of across the columns.

Figure 2.1

STATE	CITY	DEALER	MODEL	MONTH	SALES
WA	Perth	ABC Dealers	Toyota Camry	April	$46,392
WA	Perth	ABC Dealers	Toyota Camry	February	$30,224
WA	Perth	ABC Dealers	Toyota Camry	March	$58,773
WA	Perth	ABC Dealers	Toyota Camry	January	$60,382
WA	Perth	ABC Dealers	Toyota Camry	March	$62,773
WA	Perth	ABC Dealers	Toyota Camry	August	$89,399
WA	Perth	ABC Dealers	Toyota Camry	September	$25,271
WA	Perth	ABC Dealers	Land Cruiser	March	$65,605
WA	Albany	DEF Dealers	Land Cruiser	December	$65,464
WA	Albany	DEF Dealers	Land Cruiser	May	$89,114
WA	Albany	DEF Dealers	Land Cruiser	November	$24,305
WA	Albany	DEF Dealers	Land Cruiser	June	$25,875
WA	Albany	DEF Dealers	Land Cruiser	June	$44,148

Tabular layouts are akin to database layout such as SQL Server and Microsoft Access

2.1.2 DO NOT STORE DATA IN SECTION HEADINGS

Examine the data in Figure 2.2. This spreadsheet shows a report of sales of cash crops (export) by month for some West African countries. Because all the data in the report pertains to West African countries, for a visual report, it is convenient to put a single cell labelled "**West Africa**" at the top of the report as shown. This approach is effective for displaying the data, but not effective when used as a pivot table data source. Again, the label for **Cocoa** for example, is cantered in multiple cells, which is not appropriate as a pivot table data source.

Figure 2.2

	A	B	C
1			West Africa
2	Cocoa	January	$138,515
3		February	$922,273
4		March	$382,041
5		April	$115,675
6		May	$86,479
8	Coffee	January	$881,555
9		February	$51,669
10		March	$912,455
11		April	$274,090
12		May	$175,374
14	Kola	January	$72,646
15		February	$751,811
16		March	$242,381
17		April	$448,589
18		May	$269,751
20	Millet	January	$878,658
21		February	$85,048
22		March	$885,755
23		April	$477,656
24		May	$67,819

Also, the worksheet in Figure 2.2 is missing column headings. Column names are required for pivot table reports

2.1.3 AVOID REPEATING GROUPS AS COLUMNS

The format shown in Figure 2.3 is common. A time dimension is presented across several columns. This format is not ideal for a pivot table report, even though is easy to interpret. The problem is that the headings spreading across the top of the table double as column labels and actual data values. In a pivot table, this format would force you to manage and maintain six fields, each representing a different month. This arrangement will not allow you to filter the report for say June because the month of June represents a column. Instead you should create a Month field that contains the names of the months and a separate column that contains the values for each month. See section 2.1.1.

Figure 2.3

	A	B	C	D	E	F	G
1	CROP	JANUARY	FEBRUARY	MARCH	APRIL	MAY	JUNE
2	Cocoa	$3,928,020	$3,977,296	$1,489,931	$3,908,562	$3,600,332	$1,488,324
3	Cashew	$9,250,231	$3,503,524	$3,246,068	$218,737	$8,442,285	$732,763
4	Shea Butter	$1,439,790	$8,952,813	$9,033,187	$8,134,352	$2,127,549	$4,077,200
5	Millet	$1,424,883	$8,935,642	$4,752,908	$6,100,950	$6,459,701	$1,298,322
6	Soghum	$1,687,525	$4,954,924	$3,725,056	$8,085,851	$6,671,923	$9,500,728
7	Groundnuts	$839,947	$2,241,228	$4,607,076	$9,582,443	$8,500,780	$3,991,801

2.1.4 MAKE YOUR DATA SOURCE COMPACT (NO GAPS)

All cells must have values. Replace null (empty cells) with logical missing value codes such as **N/A** before attempting to create your pivot table report.

2.1.5 APPLY APPROPRIATE TYPE FORMATTING

Ensure that any field to be used in calculations are explicitly formatted as number, currency, or any other format appropriate for use in mathematical functions. Fields containing dates should also be formatted as any one of the available date formats.

2.1.6 SUMMARY OF GOOD SOURCE DATA DESIGN

The attributes of an effective tabular design are as follows:

- The first row of the data source is made up of field labels or heading that describe the information in each column

- Each column in the data source represents a unique *category* of data

- Each row in the data source represents individual items in each column

- None of the column names in the data source doubles as data items that will be used as filters or query criteria (that is, name of months, dates, years, names of locations, or country names). For example, you might want to filter the data for Australia, so "**Australia**" cannot be in the **Columns** area. Instead, use a column called "**Country**" which has Australia as one of the countries

EXERCISE 2a:

The table shown below (Figure 2.3A) is good for a visual report. However, it cannot be effectively used as a data source for a pivot table. Can you identify the problem with this data set?

Figure 2.3A

	A	B	C	D	E	F	G
1	Region	Producers		Jan	Feb	Mar	Apr
2	Coffee						
3	West Africa	Ghana		6,903	2,902	9,936	2,302
4		Ivory Coast		8,182	6,899	5,133	2,612
5		Gambia		8,829	8,973	897	1,359
6	South America	Brazil		9,630	1,438	9,811	8,902
7		Peru		5,509	7,058	2,292	5,965
8				3,914	7,155	8,323	5,861
9	Cocoa			7,419	9,405	1,420	7,841
10	West Africa	Ghana		4,145	5,614	6,785	8,166
11		Ivory Coast		7,097	2,330	529	1,374
12		Gambia		7,478	8,381	9,457	8,038
13	South America	Brazil		7,678	8,787	2,645	1,146
14		Peru		1,810	7,303	2,589	463

The above table can be restructured as follows to make it pivot table compatible. See Figure 2.3B

Figure 2.3B

Region ▼	Producer ▼	Product Category ▼	Month ▼	Tonnes ▼
West Africa	Ghana	Coffee	Jan	6,903
West Africa	Ghana	Coffee	Feb	2,902
West Africa	Ghana	Coffee	Mar	9,936
West Africa	Ghana	Coffee	Apr	2,302
West Africa	Ivory Coast	Coffee	Jan	8,182
West Africa	Ivory Coast	Coffee	Feb	6,899
West Africa	Ivory Coast	Coffee	Mar	5,133
West Africa	Ivory Coast	Coffee	Apr	2,612
West Africa	Gambia	Coffee	Jan	8,829
West Africa	Gambia	Coffee	Feb	8,973
West Africa	Gambia	Coffee	Mar	897
West Africa	Gambia	Coffee	Apr	1,359
South America	Brazil	Coffee	Jan	9,630
South America	Brazil	Coffee	Feb	1,438
South America	Brazil	Coffee	Mar	9,811
South America	Brazil	Coffee	Apr	8,902
South America	Peru	Coffee	Jan	5,509
South America	Peru	Coffee	Feb	7,058
South America	Peru	Coffee	Mar	2,292
South America	Peru	Coffee	Apr	5,965

And a pivot table on the above data will like Figure 2.3C

Figure 2.3C

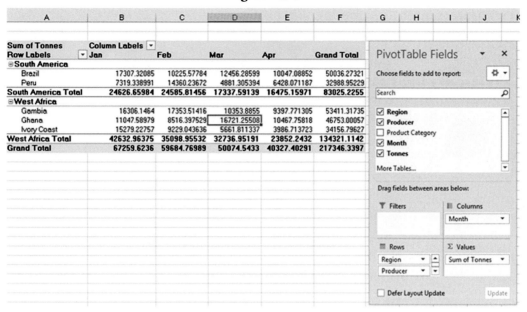

2.2 CREATING YOUR FIRST PIVOT TABLE

- Open the **CreatingPivotTable.xlsx** workbook in the exercise folder and activate the **FirstPivotTable** worksheet

- Click any single cell in the data source

- Select the **Insert ➔ Tables ➔ PivotTables**. This activates the **Create PivotTable** dialog box, shown in Figure 2.4. The Create PivotTable dialog box asks two fundamental questions:

Figure 2.4

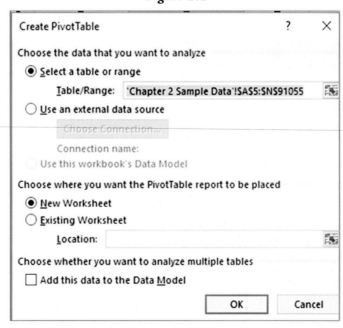

1. Choose the data set to be analysed. You can specify a data set that is located within your workbook,

or you can tell Excel to look for an external data set. Excel will highlight the dataset. However, always ensure that you are capturing all the data.

2. Choose where you want to place the pivot table

2.2.1 ADDING FIELDS TO THE REPORT

You add fields into the pivot table by using the four "**drop zones**" found in the **PivotTable Field List**. See Figure 2.4A. **Filters**, **Columns**, **Rows**, and **Values**. These four zones are used to populate the pivot table with data.

Figure 2.4A

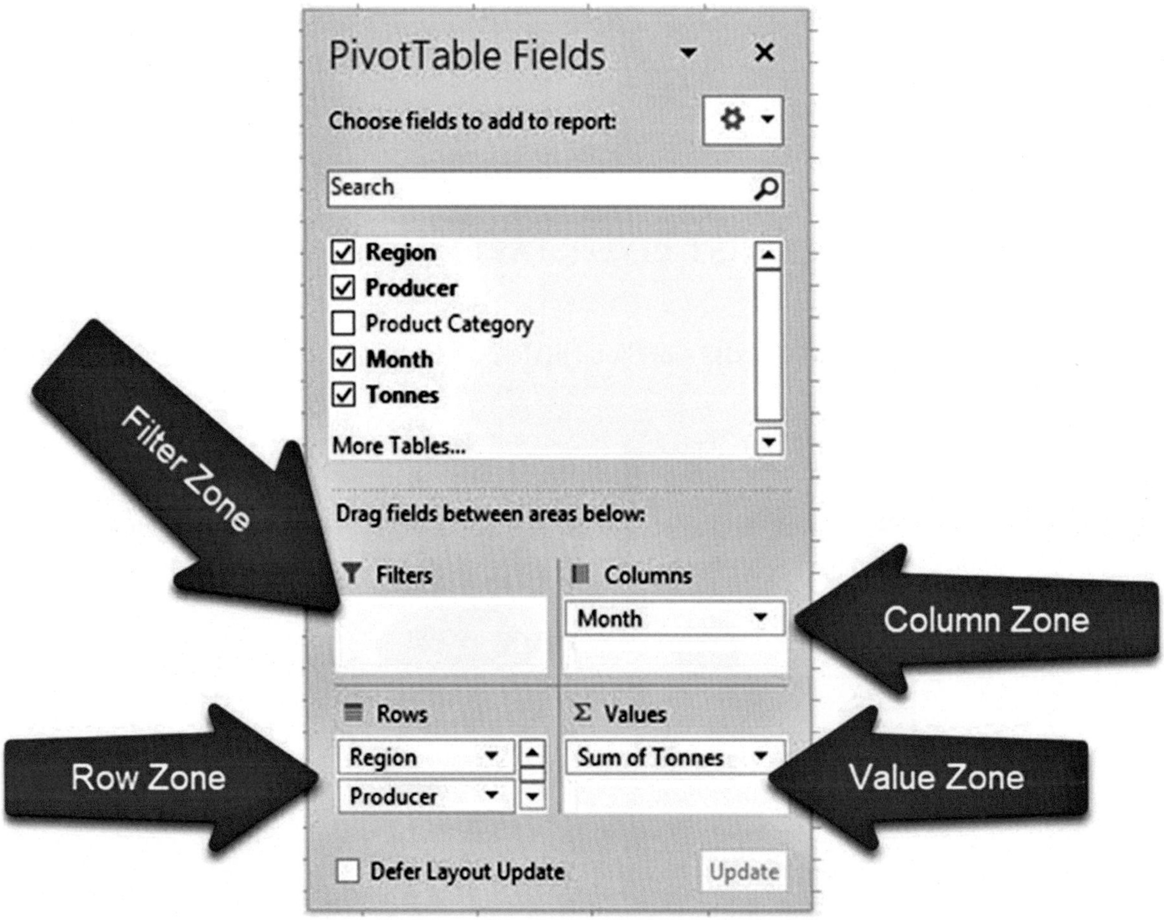

In this exercise, we want to measure the production (in tonnes) of **Coffee** and **Cocoa** by **Region** and **Month**. This tells you that you need to work with the **Tonnes**, **Region, and Month** fields:

- Drag the **Region** field to the **ROWS** drop zone

- Drag the **Tonnes** field to the **VALUES** drop zone

- Drag the Month field to the **COLUMNS** area

Figure 2.5 shows the pivot table that is created.

Figure 2.5

	A	B	C	D	E	F
1						
2	✚					
3	Sum of Tonnes	Column Labels ▼				
4	Row Labels ▼	Jan	Feb	Mar	Apr	Grand Total
5	South America	24,627	24,586	17,338	16,475	83,025
6	West Africa	42,633	35,099	32,737	23,852	134,321
7	Grand Total	67,260	59,685	50,075	40,327	217,346

2.2.2 ADDING LAYERS TO A PIVOT TABLE REPORT

We can now add another layer of analysis to the report. This time we want to measure the number of tonnes for each region by product category. Place a check mark next to the **Product Category** field. The resulting pivot table is shown in Figure 2.6. Notice the subtotals calculations for each region.

Figure 2.6

	A	B	C	D	E	F
1		✚				
2						
3	Sum of Tonnes	Column Labels ▼				
4	Row Labels ▼	Jan	Feb	Mar	Apr	Grand Total
5	⊟ South America					
6	Coffee	15,139	8,496	12,103	15,330	51,067
7	Cocoa	9,488	16,090	5,235	1,146	31,958
8	South America Total	24,627	24,586	17,338	16,475	83,025
9	⊟ West Africa					
10	Coffee	23,914	18,774	15,966	6,274	64,928
11	Cocoa	18,719	16,325	16,771	17,578	69,393
12	West Africa Total	42,633	35,099	32,737	23,852	134,321
13	Grand Total	67,260	59,685	50,075	40,327	217,346

*Note: To show the subtotals at the top of each group (instead of at the bottom as shown in Figure 2.6), place the cursor in the pivot table. In the **PivotTable Tools** group, click **Design** Then select "**Show All Subtotals at Top of Group**" from the **Subtotals** drop down*

Because the data is stored efficiently in the pivot cache, the analysis for the new pivot table took a few seconds.

2.2.3 MOVE DATA AROUND

You can rearrange the fields on the pivot table. For example, to report the **Product Category** across the top of the pivot table, simply drag the **Product Category** field from the **Rows** area into the **Columns** area, as illustrated in Figure 2.7. To make the report simpler, remove the **Month** field from the **Columns** area after you place the **Product Category** in the **Columns** area

Figure 2.7

The report is instantly restructured as shown in Figure 2.8

Figure 2.8

	A	B	C	D	E	F	G	H	I
1									
2									
3	Sum of Tonnes	Column Labels							
4		⊟Jan		⊟Feb		⊟Mar		⊞Apr	Grand Total
5	Row Labels	Coffee		Cocoa	Coffee	Cocoa	Coffee	Cocoa	
6	South America	15,139	9,488	8,496	16,090	12,103	5,235	16,475	83,025
7	West Africa	23,914	18,719	18,774	16,325	15,966	16,771	23,852	134,321
8	Grand Total	39,052	28,207	27,270	32,415	28,069	22,006	40,327	217,346

2.2.4 CREATING A REPORT FILTER

You can use the **Filter** area to create a report filter. For example, you can create a region-filtered report by simply dragging the **Region** field to the **Filters** drop zone and the **Product Category** field to the Rows drop zone. Bring the **Producer** field to the Rows zone as well to make the report more interesting. Figure 2.9 shows the report filtered for the West African region only.

Figure 2.9

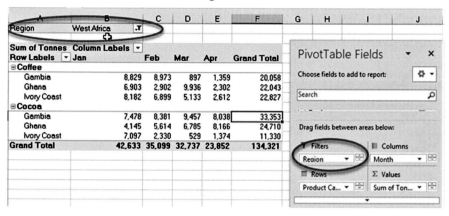

2.3 PIVOTTABLE TEMPLATES

The **Recommended PivotTable** icon, which appears next to the PivotTable icon (Figure 2.10) allows you to select from a set of predefined pivot tables that Excel suggests for you based on your data.

Figure 2.10

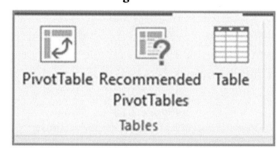

Another way to get to the Recommended pivot table is to right-click anywhere in your data range and choose the **Quick Analysis** option. The context menu shown in Figure 2.11 activates, and you can select a recommended pivot table under the **Table** section.

Figure 2.11

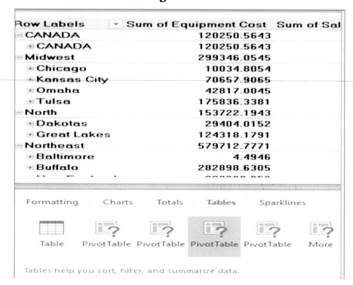

2.4 SLICERS, WHAT ARE THEY?

Slicers enable pivot tables to be filtered, like the way Filter fields are used. Slicers are however more user friendly and visual.

2.4.1 CREATING A STANDARD SLICER

To create a slicer:

• Place the cursor anywhere inside the pivot table

• Select the **Insert** tab on the ribbon. Click the **Slicer** icon (see Figure 2.12)

Figure 2.12

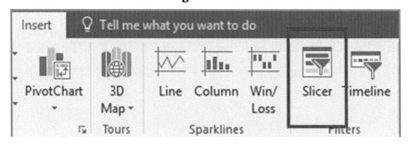

The **Insert Slicer** dialog shown in Figure 2.13 opens for you to select the dimensions you want to filter for. In this example, the **Region** and **Producers** dimensions are selected

Figure 2.13

After the slicers are created, you can simply click the filtering criteria to filter your pivot table. As Figure 2.14 illustrates, clicking **South America** in the Region slicer not only filters the pivot table, but the **Producer** slicer responds by highlighting the producers that belong to the **South America** region.

Figure 2.14

	A	B	C	D	E	F	G	H	I
1									
2									
3	Sum of Tonnes	Column Labels ▼					Region ▤ ▼		
4	Row Labels ▼	Jan	Feb	Mar	Apr	Grand Total	South America		
5	⊟ Coffee						West Africa		
6	Brazil	9,630	1,438	9,811	8,902	29,780			
7	Peru	5,509	7,058	2,292	6,428	21,286			
8	⊟ Cocoa						Producer ▤ ▼		
9	Brazil	7,678	8,787	2,645	1,146	20,256	Brazil		
10	Peru	1,810	7,303	2,589		11,703	Peru		
11	Grand Total	24,627	24,586	17,338	16,475	83,025	Gambia		
12							Ghana		
13									
14							Ivory Coast		
15									
16									
17									
18									

You can connect a slicer to more than one pivot table by right-clicking the slicer and selecting **Report Connections**. The Report Connections dialog box (Figure 2.15) opens. Place a check next to any pivot table that you want to filter using the current slicer. At this point, any filter applied via the slicer is applied to all connected pivot tables.

Exercise 2a:

Use the CreatingPivotTable.xls workbook to create multiple pivot table driven by a single slicer.

1. Open the CreatingPivotTable.xlsx and use the *Sample Data* worksheet to create a pivot table:

   a. Select a cell in the data

   b. In the Insert tab, click the Pivot Table tab

   c. Drag the Region field to the Rows drop zone

   d. Drag the Sales Amount field to the Value drop down zone

2. Select the entire pivot table and copy (Ctrl+C)

3. Paste the copied pivot table in a new blank area of the worksheet. This creates a second pivot table. Both pivot tables share a common cache. For a single slicer to run multiple pivot tables, they must share the same pivot cache

4. Change the fields in the second pivot table to show some other interesting analysis

5. Repeat steps 2-4 to create a third copy of the pivot table.

6. Create a column chart based on the third pivot table:

a. Select the pivot table

b. Select Insert. In the Charts group, select "Recommended Charts"

c. Select Clustered Column

7. Select a cell in the first pivot table. Choose **Insert Slicer**. Choose one or more fields to be used as a slicer. Alternatively, insert a timeline for a date field

8. At this point the slicer is driving only the first pivot table

9. Click the slicer to select it. When the slicer is selected, the **Slicer Tools Options** tab of the ribbon appears

10. Select the **Slicer Tools Options** tab and choose **Report Connections**. Excel displays the **Report Connection (Market)** dialog. Initially only the first pivot table is selected

11. As shown in Figure 2-15, choose the other pivot tables in the dialog and click OK

12. If you created multiple slicers and /or timelines in step 7, repeat steps 10 and 11 for the other slicers

Note: You can rename your pivot table by placing the cursor inside the pivot table, selecting the Analyse tab, and entering a name in the PivotTable Name input box found on the far left

Figure 2.15

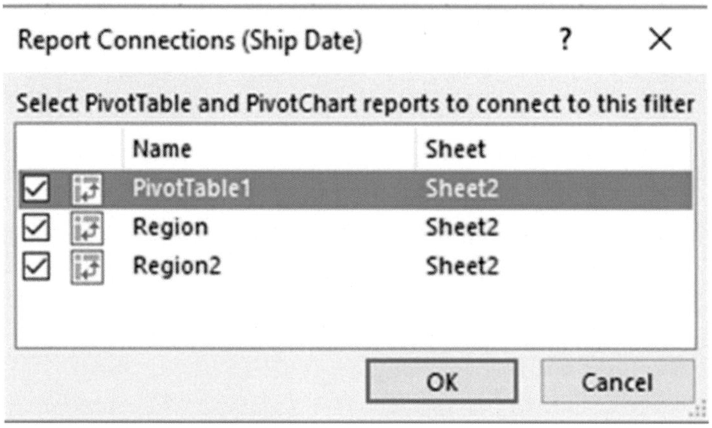

2.4.2 SLICER CAN USE DATES

From this point on until further notice, discussions are based on the "Sample Data" worksheet in the CreatingPivotTable.xlsx workbook

A **Timeline slicer** is designed to work exclusively with date fields, providing a visual method to filter and group the dates in the pivot table. For a Timeline slicer to work, all the values in the date field must be formatted as a ***valid*** date (no blank cells).

To create a Timeline slicer, place the cursor inside the pivot table, select the **Insert** tab on the ribbon, and click the Timeline icon (see Figure 2.16).

Figure 2.16

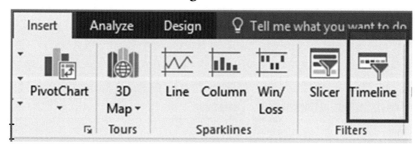

The **Insert Timeline** dialog seen in Figure 2.17 opens, showing all the available date fields in the data. Here, you select the date fields for which you want to create slicers. After the Timeline slicer is created, you can filter the data in the pivot table by using this dynamic data-selection mechanism. As shown in figure 2.18, the data has been filtered for data from February 2007 to April 2007.

Figure 2.17

Figure 2.18

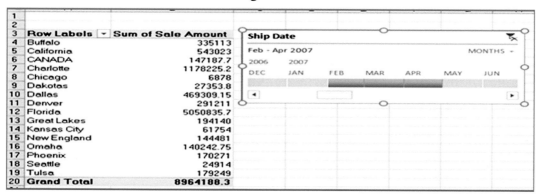

Figure 2.19

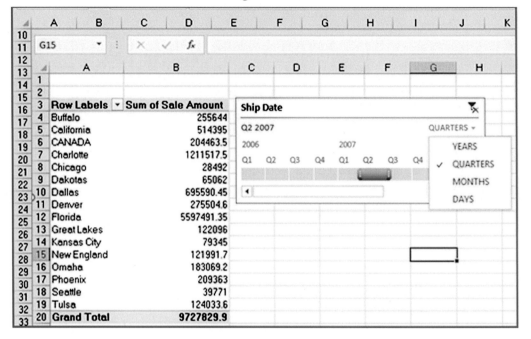

Figure 2.19 shows how you filter by **Years, Quarters, Months**, and days. Click the time period dropdown and select the appropriate time interval. In Figure 2.19, the pivot table is filtered by Quarter 2 of 2007.

Exercise 2b:

You are building a pivot table based on a dataset with over 91,000 rows. The Market field contains over 18 unique markets that sell seven types of products. Your report should break out each market and highlight the dollar sales by each product (Use the Sample Data worksheet in the CreatingPivotTable.xlsx workbook)

2.5 REFRESHING THE PIVOT TABLE REPORT

Because the pivot cache is detached from the source data, any updates to the source data are not automatically reflected in the pivot table. You need to manually refresh the pivot cache to update the pivot table. There are two reasons that call for a refresh of the pivot table report:

- When the data source changes

- New rows are added

2.5.1 WHEN THE EXISTING DATA SOURCE CHANGES

If a few cells in the data source have changed due to edits or updates, you can refresh the pivot table report by right-clicking inside the pivot table and selecting **Refresh**. This takes another snapshot of the data set overwriting the previous pivot cache with the latest data

2.5.2 WHEN ROWS AND COLUMNS EXPAND AND SHRINK

When the range of the pivot table data source changes (addition of columns or rows), you have to update the range by doing the following:

- Click anywhere inside the pivot table

- Select **PivotTable Tools, Analyse → Change Data Source** (see Figure 2.20).

Figure 2.20

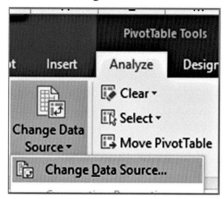

- The dialog box shown in Figure 2.21 is shown

Figure 2.21

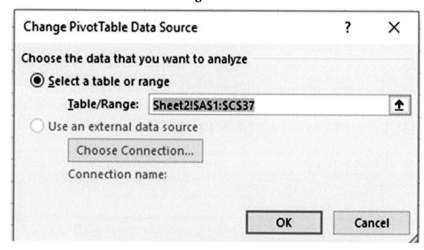

- Use the **Table/Range** text box to adjust the data source range.

2.6 A LOOK AT THE NEW PIVOT TABLE TOOLS

The following sections look at a few of the tools that help to save time with pivot table management

2.6.1 SUSPENDING UPDATES

Excel 2013 & 2016 offer a way to delay automatic analysis of a pivot table whenever a new field is added to the pivot area. This action can be activated by clicking the **Defer Layout Update** check box in the **PivotTable Field List** dialog, as shown in Figure 2.22

Figure 2.22

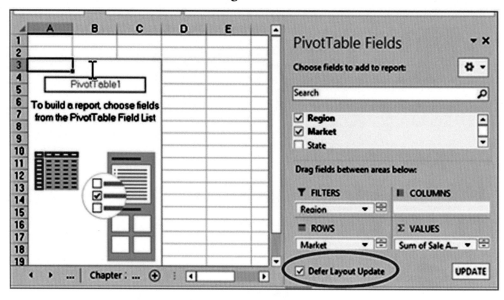

When you place a check in the **Defer Layout Update** check box, you prevent the pivot table from making immediate updates as you move your fields around within your pivot table. In Figure 2.22, notice that fields in the drop zones are not in the pivot table yet. When it is time to apply the changes, click the **Update** button on the lower-right corner of the **PivotTable Field List** dialog.

2.6.2 CLEAR THE PIVOT TABLE REPORT

To clear the pivot table and start from scratch, choose **PivotTable Tools → Analyse** (Figure 2.23)

Figure 2.23

You can either choose to remove the entire pivot table layout or remove any applied filter

2.6.3 RELOCATING THE PIVOT TABLE

Using the **Clear** dropdown in the **Actions** group, you can relocate pivot table report by choosing **PivotTable Tools → Analyse → Move PivotTable** to open the **Move PivotTable** dialog illustrated in Figure 2.24

Figure 2.24

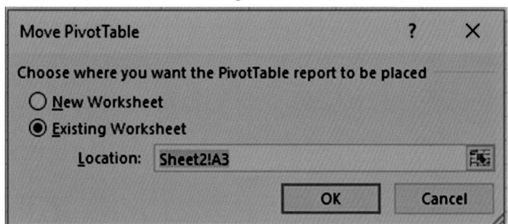

3. CUSTOMIZING YOUR PIVOT TABLE REPORT

Many customizations can be applied to a pivot table report, such as layout changes, major and advanced calculations and other visualization enhancement changes.

3.1 ENHANCING THE PIVOT TABLE REPORT

Figure 3.1 shows a typical pivot table. To create this pivot table, open the **EnhancePT.xlsx** workbook and open the **Exporters** worksheet. Select **Insert**, **PivotTable**, **OK**. Check the **Export Revenue** to place it in the VALUES zone, move the **Crop** to the ROWS zone and **Month** to the COLUMNS zone

Figure 3.1

	A	B	C	D	E	F	G	H
1								
2								
3	Sum of Export Revenue	Column Labels ▾						
4	Row Labels ▾	January	February	March	April	Mar	Apr	Grand Total
5	Cashew		$25,393,609					$25,393,609
6	Cocoa	$18,392,465						$18,392,465
7	Groundnuts						$29,763,274	$29,763,274
8	Millet			$28,972,404				$28,972,404
9	Shea Butter					$33,764,891		$33,764,891
10	Soghum				$34,626,007			$34,626,007
11	Grand Total	$18,392,465	$25,393,609	$28,972,404	$34,626,007	$33,764,891	$29,763,274	$170,912,650

3.1.1 USING THE TABLE STYLE FEATURES

The default pivot table has no gridlines. Follow these steps to apply a style to restore gridlines:

1. Select a cell within the pivot table

2. From the **Ribbon**, select **Design** tab

3. Three arrows appear at the right side of the **PivotTable Style** gallery. Click the bottom arrow to open the complete gallery, which is shown in Figure 3.2

Figure 3.2

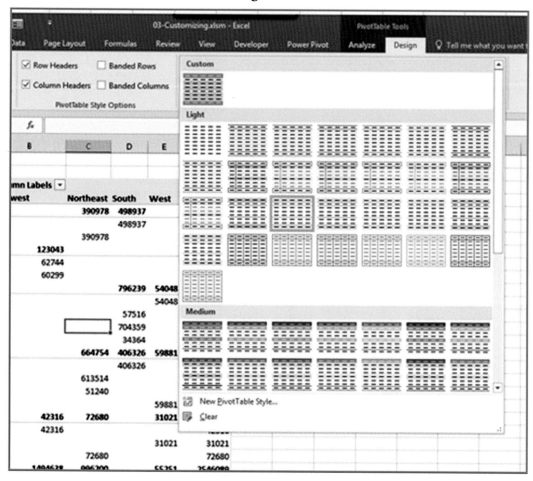

4. Choose any style other than the first style from the drop-down

5. Select the check box for Banded Rows to the left of the PivotTable Style gallery

6. You may choose to apply banded columns as well

3.1.2 FORMATTING NUMBERS

You can apply number formatting to the pivot table by using the **Number Format** in the **Value Field Setting** dialog. There are three ways to get to this dialog box:

- Right-click a number in the VALUES area of the pivot table and select **Value Field Setting**

- Click the dropdown on the **Sum of Export Revenue** field in the drop zones of the PivotTable Field List and then select **Value Field Settings** from the context menu

- Select any cell in the VALUES area of the pivot table. From the **Analyse** tab, select **Field Settings** from the **Active Field** group. As shown in Figure 3.3, the **Value Field Settings** dialog box is displayed. To change the numeric format, click the **Number Format** button in the lower-left corner. In the **Format Cell** dialog, you can choose any built-in number format or choose a custom format. For example, choose **Currency**, as shown in Figure 3.4

Figure 3.3

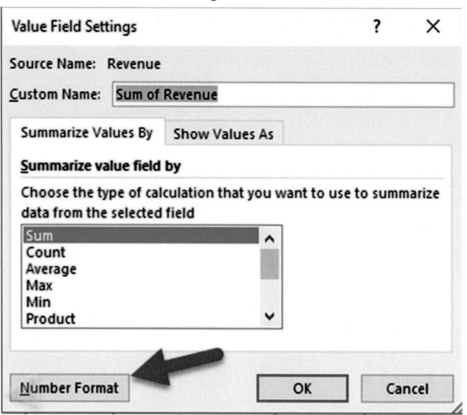

Figure 3.4

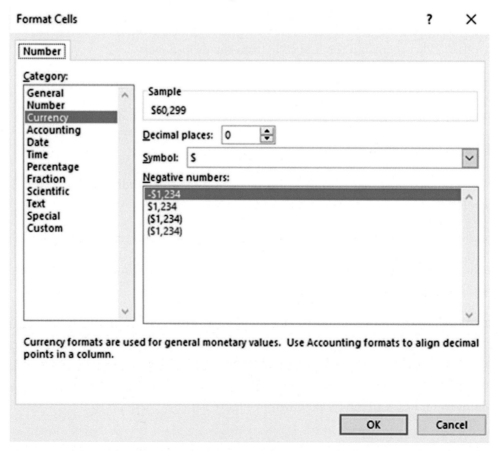

3.1.3 REPLACING BLANK VALUES WITH ZEROS

It is a good spreadsheet design not to leave blank cells in a numeric section of the worksheet. Even a single blank cell in a numeric column will produce a **Count** aggregate instead of **Sum** in the pivot table. For example, if you leave one or more empty rows between the data headers and the main dataset, you will receive "**Blank**" as a group in your analysis. In addition, the "**Count**" aggregation will automatically be applied. The blank indicates that there were no sales for that particular combination of labels. Use the following steps to change the settings for the current pivot table:

1. Right-click any cell in the pivot table and choose **PivotTable Options**

2. On the **Layout & Format** tab, in the Format section, type **0** next to the field labelled **For Empty Cells Show** (see Figure 3.5)

3. Click **OK** to accept the change

The result is that the pivot table blank values are replaced with zeros, as shown in figure 3.6

Figure 3.5

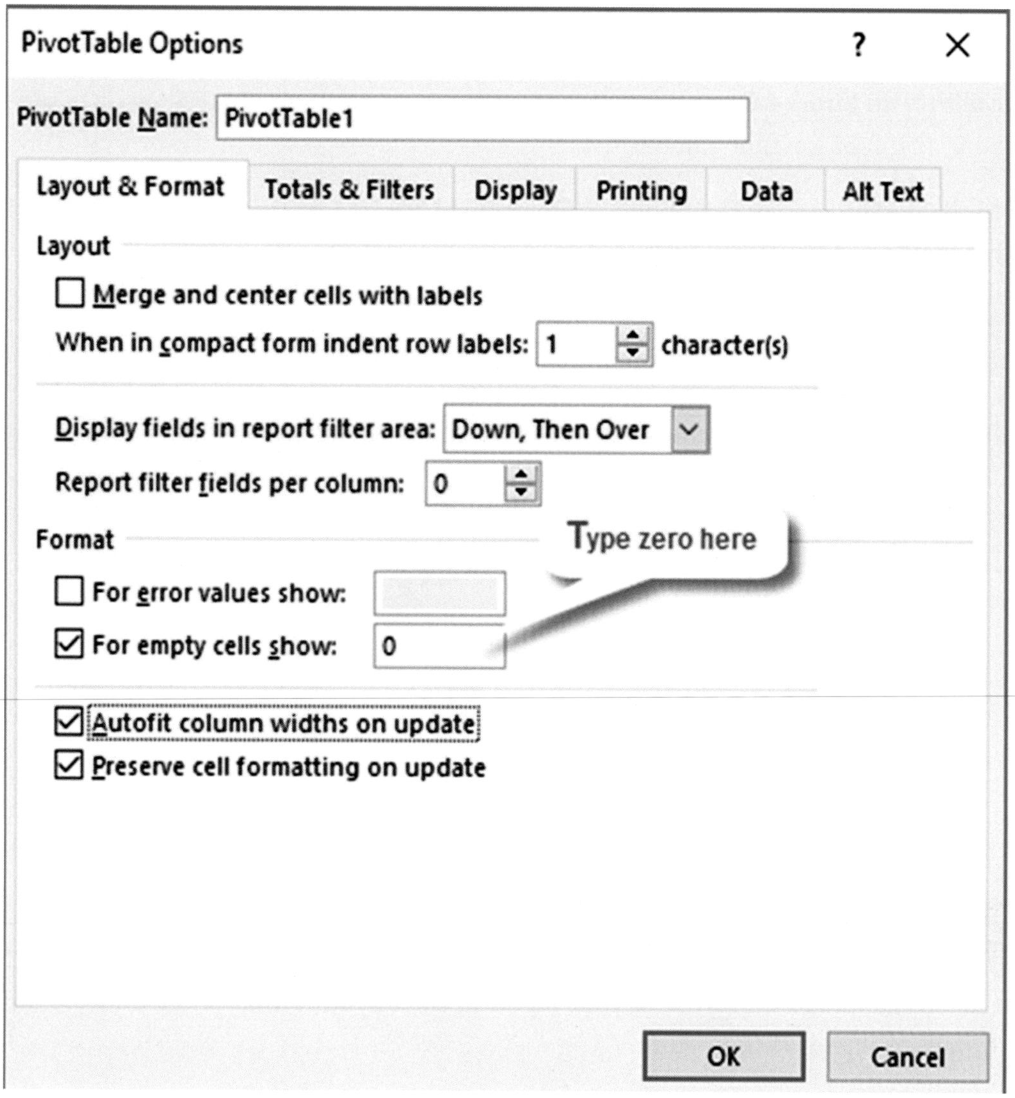

Figure 3.6

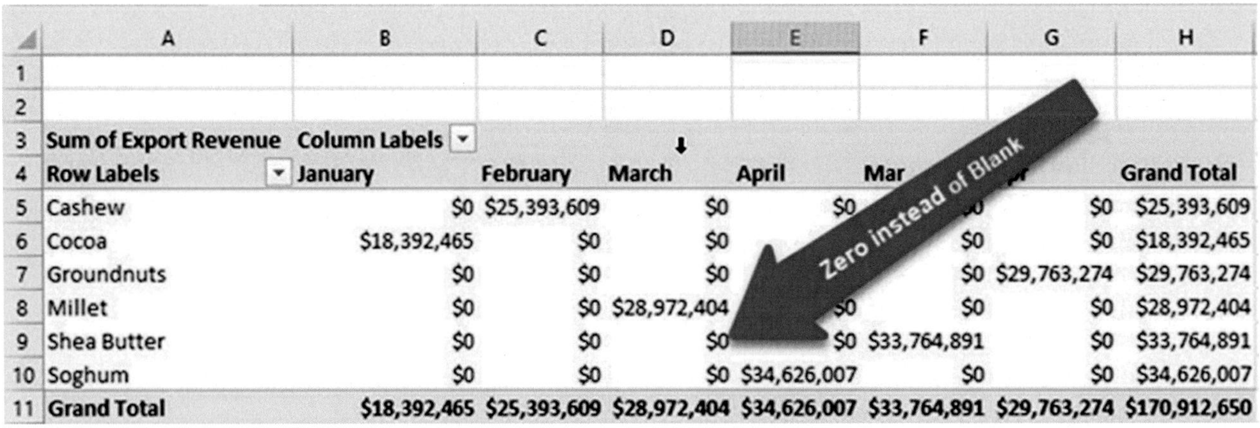

	A	B	C	D	E	F	G	H
1								
2								
3	Sum of Export Revenue	Column Labels ▾			↓			
4	Row Labels ▾	January	February	March	April	Mar		Grand Total
5	Cashew	$0	$25,393,609	$0	$0		$0	$25,393,609
6	Cocoa	$18,392,465	$0	$0		$0	$0	$18,392,465
7	Groundnuts	$0	$0	$0			$0	$29,763,274	$29,763,274
8	Millet	$0	$0	$28,972,404		$0	$0	$0	$28,972,404
9	Shea Butter	$0	$0	$0	$0	$33,764,891	$0	$33,764,891
10	Soghum	$0	$0	$0	$34,626,007	$0	$0	$34,626,007
11	Grand Total	$18,392,465	$25,393,609	$28,972,404	$34,626,007	$33,764,891	$29,763,274	$170,912,650

Zero instead of Blank

3.1.4 CHANGING A FIELD NAME

Fields in **Row**, **Column** and **Filter** areas inherit their names from their headings in the source data. Fields in the data section are given names such as **Sum of Revenue**. To change a field name in the VALUES area, follow these steps:

1. Select a cell in the pivot table that contains the appropriate type of value. You might have a pivot table with both **Sum of Quantity** and **Sum of Revenue** in the **VALUES** area. Choose a cell that contains a Sum of Revenue value

2. Go to the **Analyse** tab in the ribbon. A **Pivot Field Name** text box appears below the heading of **Active Field**

3. Type a new name in the box, as shown in Figure 3.7

Figure 3.7

3.2 MAKING CHANGES TO REPORT LAYOUT

You can make changes to the layout of your report in the **Layout** group of the **Design** tab, as shown in Figure 3.8. This group offers four icons:

• **Subtotals** – Moves subtotals to the top or bottom of each group or turns them off

- **Grand Totals** – Turns the grand totals on or off for rows and columns

- **Report Layout** – Uses the Compact, Outline, or Tabular forms. Offers the option to repeat item labels

- **Blank Rows** – Insert or removes blank lines after each group

Figure 3.8

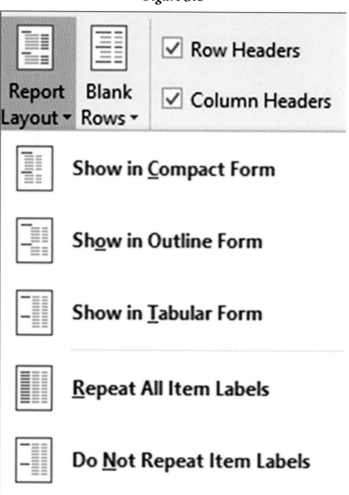

3.2.1 USING THE COMPACT LAYOUT

By default, all new pivot tables use the **Compact** layout shown in Figure 3.9. In this layout, multiple fields in the row area are stacked in first column. Note in the figure that the **Crop** and the **Producer** countries are both in the first column. The Compact form is suited for using the **Expand** and **Collapse** icons. Select one of the Crop value cells such as **Cashew** in the first column. Click the **Expand Field** icon on the **Analyse** tab. Excel expands the list and shows all the Cashew producing countries, as shown in Figure 3.9. After a field is expanded, you can hide detail items by using the minus icons attached to the item. In Figure 3.9, the **Cashew** crop is expanded to show its producers.

Figure 3.9

Row Labels	January	February	March	April	Mar	Apr	Grand Total
⊟ Cashew	$0	$25,393,609	$0	$0	$0	$0	$25,393,609
Gambia	$0	$732,763	$0	$0	$0	$0	$732,763
Ghana	$0	$9,250,231	$0	$0	$0	$0	$9,250,231
Ivory Coast	$0	$218,737	$0	$0	$0	$0	$218,737
Mali	$0	$8,442,285	$0	$0	$0	$0	$8,442,285
Nigeria	$0	$3,503,524	$0	$0	$0	$0	$3,503,524
Togo	$0	$3,246,068	$0	$0	$0	$0	$3,246,068
⊞ Cocoa	$18,392,465	$0	$0	$0	$0	$0	$18,392,465
⊞ Groundnuts	$0	$0	$0	$0	$0	$29,763,274	$29,763,274
⊞ Millet	$0	$0	$28,972,404	$0	$0	$0	$28,972,404
⊞ Shea Butter	$0	$0	$0	$0	$33,764,891	$0	$33,764,891
⊞ Soghum	$0	$0	$0	$34,626,007	$0	$0	$34,626,007
Grand Total	$18,392,465	$25,393,609	$28,972,404	$34,626,007	$33,764,891	$29,763,274	$170,912,650

To get the above pivot table, use the **EnhancePT.xlsx** workbook. Place the **Crop** and **Producer** fields in the ROWS zone, the **Month** field in the COLUMNS zone and the **Export Revenue** field in the VALUES zone

3.2.2 USING THE OUTLINE FORM LAYOUT

The **Outline Form** layout puts each row field in a separate column as illustrated by Figure 3.10. If you choose "**Repeat All Item Labels**" (**Design → Report Layout**), all the blanks cells will be filled with labels. For example, the empty cells below the "**Cashew**" cell (within the red box) will all be filled with the word "**Cashew**". See Figure 3.10A. This layout is appropriate if you plan to copy the pivot table report to a different area for further analysis. You can use the **Subtotals** dropdown on the **Design** tab to relocate the subtotals to the top or bottom of each column.

Figure 3.10

CROP	Producer	January	February	March	April	Mar	Apr	Grand Total
⊟ Cashew		$0	$25,393,609	$0	$0	$0	$0	$25,393,609
	Gambia	$0	$732,763	$0	$0	$0	$0	$732,763
	Ghana	$0	$9,250,231	$0	$0	$0	$0	$9,250,231
	Ivory Coast	$0	$218,737	$0	$0	$0	$0	$218,737
	Mali	$0	$8,442,285	$0	$0	$0	$0	$8,442,285
	Nigeria	$0	$3,503,524	$0	$0	$0	$0	$3,503,524
	Togo	$0	$3,246,068	$0	$0	$0	$0	$3,246,068
⊞ Cocoa		$18,392,465	$0	$0	$0	$0	$0	$18,392,465
⊟ Groundnuts		$0	$0	$0	$0	$0	$29,763,274	$29,763,274
Groundnuts	Gambia	$0	$0	$0	$0	$0	$3,991,801	$3,991,801
Groundnuts	Ghana	$0	$0	$0	$0	$0	$839,947	$839,947
Groundnuts	Ivory Coast	$0	$0	$0	$0	$0	$9,582,443	$9,582,443
Groundnuts	Mali	$0	$0	$0	$0	$0	$8,500,780	$8,500,780
Groundnuts	Nigeria	$0	$0	$0	$0	$0	$2,241,228	$2,241,228
Groundnuts	Togo	$0	$0	$0	$0	$0	$4,607,076	$4,607,076
⊞ Millet		$0	$0	$28,972,404	$0	$0	$0	$28,972,404
⊞ Shea Butter		$0	$0	$0	$0	$33,764,891	$0	$33,764,891
⊞ Soghum		$0	$0	$0	$34,626,007	$0	$0	$34,626,007
Grand Total		$18,392,465	$25,393,609	$28,972,404	$34,626,007	$33,764,891	$29,763,274	$170,912,650

3.2.3 USING THE TABULAR LAYOUT

The **Tabular** layout is the best layout if you expect to use the resulting summary data in a subsequent analysis. To reuse the table in Figure 3.10, will require additional "flattening" of the pivot table by choosing **Subtotals Do Not Show Subtotals** and **Grand Totals Off for Rows and Columns**.

Figure 3.10A

	A	B	C	D	E	F	G	H	I
4	CROP ▼	Producer ▼	January	February	March	April	Mar	Apr	Grand Total
5	⊟ Cashew	Gambia	$0	$732,763	$0	$0	$0	$0	$732,763
6	Cashew	Ghana	$0	$9,250,231	$0	$0	$0	$0	$9,250,231
7	Cashew	Ivory Coast	$0	$218,737	$0	$0	$0	$0	$218,737
8	Cashew	Mali	$0	$8,442,285	$0	$0	$0	$0	$8,442,285
9	Cashew	Nigeria	$0	$3,503,524	$0	$0	$0	$0	$3,503,524
10	Cashew	Togo	$0	$3,246,068	$0	$0	$0	$0	$3,246,068
11	Cashew Total		$0	$25,393,609	$0	$0	$0	$0	$25,393,609
12	⊞ Cocoa		$18,392,465	$0	$0	$0	$0	$0	$18,392,465
13	⊟ Groundnuts	Gambia	$0	$0	$0		$3,991,801		$3,991,801
14	Groundnuts	Ghana	$0	$0	$0			$839,947	$839,947
15	Groundnuts	Ivory Coast	$0	$0	$0			$9,582,443	$9,582,443
16	Groundnuts	Mali	$0	$0	$0	$0		$8,500,780	$8,500,780
17	Groundnuts	Nigeria	$0	$0	$0	$0	$0	$2,241,228	$2,241,228
18	Groundnuts	Togo	$0	$0	$0	$0	$0	$4,607,076	$4,607,076
19	Groundnuts Total		$0	$0	$0	$0	$0	$29,763,274	$29,763,274
20	⊞ Millet		$0	$0	$28,972,404	$0	$0	$0	$28,972,404
21	⊞ Shea Butter		$0	$0	$0	$0	$33,764,891	$0	$33,764,891
22	⊞ Soghum		$0	$0	$0	$34,626,007	$0	$0	$34,626,007
23	Grand Total		$18,392,465	$25,393,609	$28,972,404	$34,626,007	$33,764,891	$29,763,274	$170,912,650

(Callout box: Sum of Export Revenue — Value: $0 — Row: Cocoa — Column: April)

3.2.4 BLANK LINES, GRAND TOTALS, AND OTHER SETTINGS

The **Blank Rows** dropdown on the **Design** tab offers a choice for **Insert Blank Row After Each Item**. The blank row would be added after each group of items in the outer row fields.

Grand Totals may appear at the bottom of each column and or at the end of each row, or they can be turned off altogether. Settings for grand totals appear in the **Grand Totals** dropdown of the **Layout** group on the **Design** tab as shown in Figure 3.11

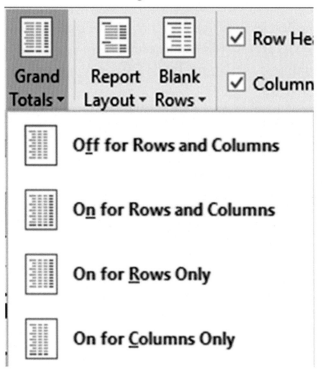

Figure 3.11

3.3 ENHANCE YOUR REPORT WITH STYLES AND THEMES

You can quickly apply colour and formatting to the pivot table report using the 85-built-in style in the **PivotTable Style** gallery on the **Design** tab. You can start with the four check boxes in the **PivotTable Style Options** group of the **Desi**gn tab of the Ribbon as shown in Figure 3.12.

Figure 3.12

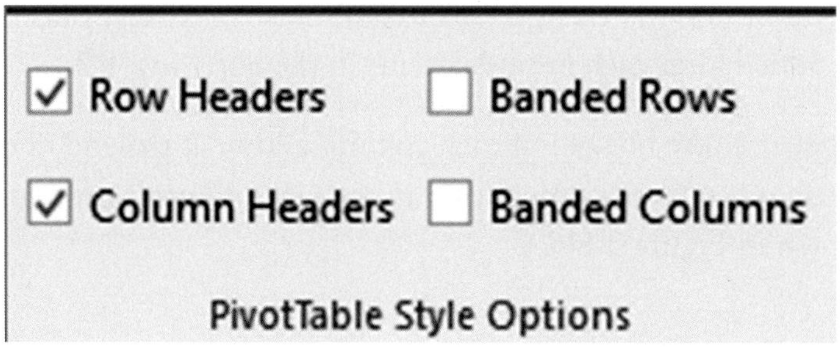

✓ Row Headers ☐ Banded Rows

✓ Column Headers ☐ Banded Columns

PivotTable Style Options

You can choose to apply special formatting to the row headers, column headers, banded rows, or banded columns. Choices on the **PivotTable Style Option** modify the thumbnails shown in the **PivotTable Styles** gallery

3.3.1 CREATING CUSTOM STYLES

You can create new styles of your own which are added to the gallery for the current workbook only. To use the custom style in another workbook, copy and temporarily paste the formatted pivot table to the other workbook. The pivot table carries its formatting to the other workbook. After the pivot table has been pasted, apply the custom style to an existing pivot table in the workbook and then delete the temporarily pivot table that you pasted.

To create a custom pivot table style in which the banded colours are three rows high, for example, follow these steps:

1. Click a cell within the pivot table and select **PivotTable Tools → Design**

2. Select the **Banded Rows** check-box in the **PivotTables Style Options** group. This highlights the banded row styles in the gallery

3. Right-click a style in the gallery that supports banded rows and select **Duplicate**. Excel displays the **Modify PivotTable** dialog. See Fig. 3-13

4. Give the custom style a name, such as **MyCustomStyle**

5. In the **Table Element** list, click **First Row Stripe**. A new section called **Stripe Size** appears in the dialog

6. Select 3 from the Stripe Size dropdown, as shown in Figure 3.13

Figure 3.13

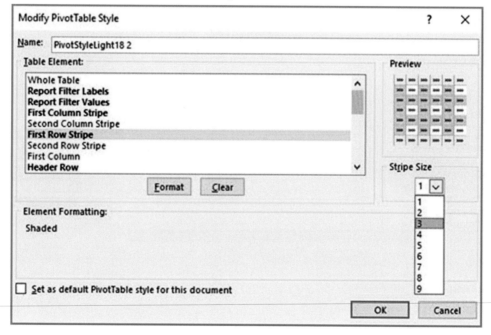

7. To change the stripe colour, click the Format button. The Format Cells dialog appears. Click the Fill tab and then choose a Fill Colour. You can use the More Colours button to define your own colour. Click OK to return to Modify PivotTables Style dialog

8. In the Table Element List, click Second Row Stripe. Change the Strip Size dropdown to 3. Modify the format to use a lighter colour such as white

9. You can choose to save the custom pivot table style as default for the workbook

10. Optionally edit the colours for the Header Row and Grand Total Row

11. Click OK to finish building the style

12. The new style should be in the first thumbnail visible in the style gallery. Click the custom style to apply it to the pivot table.

Exercise 3A: Creating and Applying Custom Style

1. Open the CustomizingPT.xlsx workbook

2. Use the "Data" worksheet to create a pivot table in a new worksheet

    a. Place the **Region** and **Customer** fields in the **Rows** zone in that order

    b. Place the **Revenue**, **Profit** and **Cost** field in the **Values** zone

3. Click any cell in the pivot table and select **PivotTableTools Design**

4. Continue, using steps 2 through 12 of section 3.3.1 to create a custom style

5. In step 4 use your first name for the custom style name

6. Apply any colour to the Header and the **GrandTotal** rows as shown below

Figure 3.14

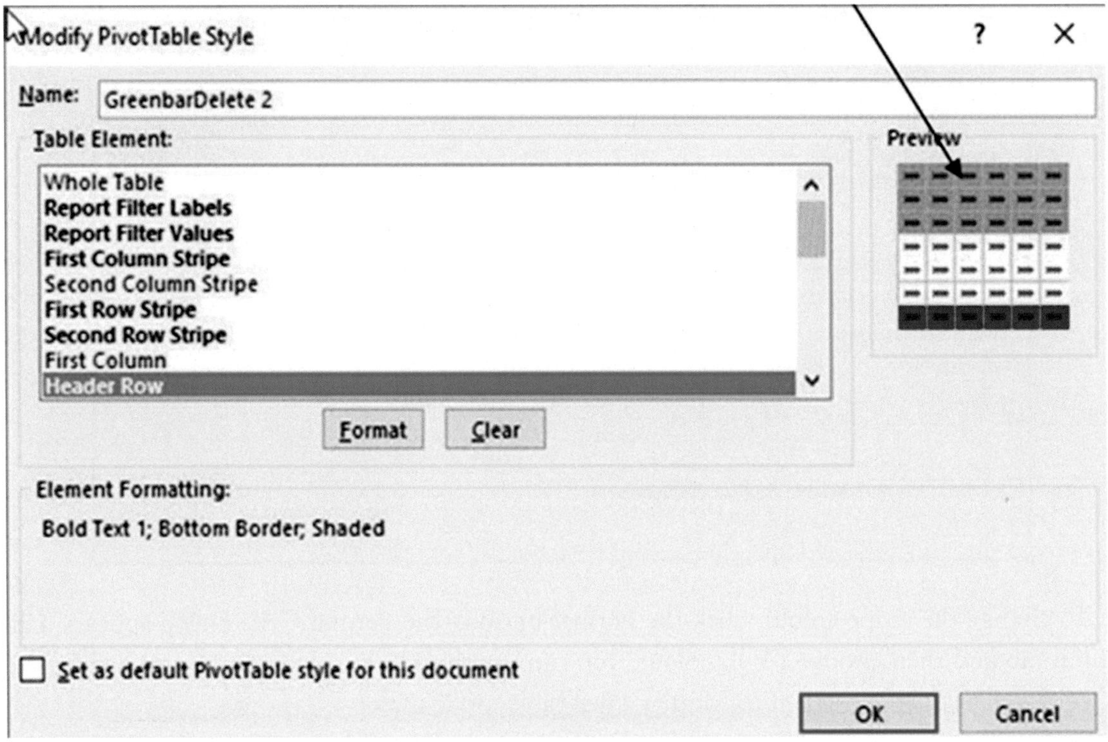

7. Now apply the custom format to a new pivot table in a different workbook

    a. Open the CustomStyle.xlsx workbook

    b. Use the Data worksheet to create a pivot table as follows:

    i.   **Row Zone**: Region and Market fields

    ii. **Column Zone**: Year field

    iii. Value Zone: SalesAmount field

c. Copy the first (formatted) pivot table. To copy the pivot table, place the cursor in the pivot table and click Ctrl + A

d. Paste it in the worksheet beside the second pivot table. The pivot table will come with the custom format. This will make the custom format available for the new pivot table.

e. Select the second pivot table. Verify that your custom style is in the styles gallery (in the **PivotTable Styles** group)

f. Apply the style to the new pivot table and delete the one you pasted.

This technique ensures that you create a custom style once and apply it to various pivot tables

3.4 APPLYING DIFFERENT AGGREGATION FUNCTIONS

By default, Excel summarizes pivot table data by either counting (when there is an empty cell value or a text value in place of a number) or summing the items. Instead of **Sum** or **Count**, you might want to choose functions such as **Min, Max, and Count Numeric**. In all 11 options are available.

Excel gives you other aggregate functions through the **Summarize Values By** command, plus five more options when you select **More Options**. The options available are:

- **Sum** – Provides a total of all numeric data

- **Count** – Counts all cells, including numeric, text, and error cells. This is equivalent to the Excel function **COUNTA ()**

- **Average** – Provides an average

- **Max** – Shows the largest value

- **Min** – Shows the smallest value

- **Product** – Multiplies all the cells together. For example, if your data set has cells with values 3, 4, and 5, the product would be 60

- **Count Nums** – Counts only the numeric cells. This is equivalent to Excel's **COUNT** function

- **StdDev and StdDevP** – Calculates the standard deviation. Use StdDevP if your data set contains the complete population. Use StdDev if your data set contains a sample of the population

- **Var and varP** – Calculates the statistical variance

3.5 DISPLAYING AND SUPPRESSING SUBTOTALS

In pivot tables, you can display or suppress the display of subtotals

3.5.1 REMOVE SUBTOTALS

When you have many unique rows, subtotals can mire the view.

For example, in Figure 3.15, there is no need to show subtotals for each Crop because there is only one Rep for each crop

Figure 3.15

	A	B	C	D
1				
2				
3	**Producer** ▼	**CROP** ▼	**Rep** ▼	**Sum of Export Revenue**
4	⊟ Gambia	⊟ Cashew	Sam	732763.3692
5		**Cashew Total**		**732763.3692**
6		⊟ Cocoa	Mike	1488324.143
7		**Cocoa Total**		**1488324.143**
8		⊟ Groundnuts	Chris	3991800.773
9		**Groundnuts Total**		**3991800.773**
10		⊟ Millet	Danielle	1298322.1
11		**Millet Total**		**1298322.1**
12		⊟ Shea Butter	Paul	4077200.277
13		**Shea Butter Total**		**4077200.277**
14		⊟ Soghum	David	9500728.234
15		**Soghum Total**		**9500728.234**
16	**Gambia Total**			**21089138.9**
17	⊞ Ghana			18570395.02
18	⊞ Ivory Coast			36030894.53
19	⊞ Mali			35802570.16
20	⊞ Nigeria			32565426.4
21	⊞ Togo			26854225.3
22	**Grand Total**			**170912650.3**

Create this pivot table in the EnhancePT_A.xlsx workbook. Use the Export worksheet. Use the Producer, Crop, and Rep fields in the Rows zone. Use the Export Revenue field in the Values zone. Apply the Outline Form layout

If you used the **Subtotals** dropdown on the **Design** tab, you would turn off all subtotals, including the **Producer** subtotals and the **Crop** subtotals. The Producer subtotals are still providing good information, so you want to use the **Subtotals** setting in the **Field Settings** dialog. Choose one of the cells in the **Crop** column. On the Analyse tab, choose **Field Settings**. Change the **Subtotals** settings from **Automatic** to **None.** This removes the subtotals for only the **Rep** field and leaves the subtotals for the Producer field intact

3.5.2 MULTIPLE SUBTOTALS FOR A SINGLE FIELD

You can add customized subtotals to a row or column label fields. Select the **Producer** field in the bottom of the **Pivot Table Field List** and select **Field Settings**. Select **Custom** and then select the type of subtotal you want. The next figure shows five custom subtotals selected for the **Producer** field.

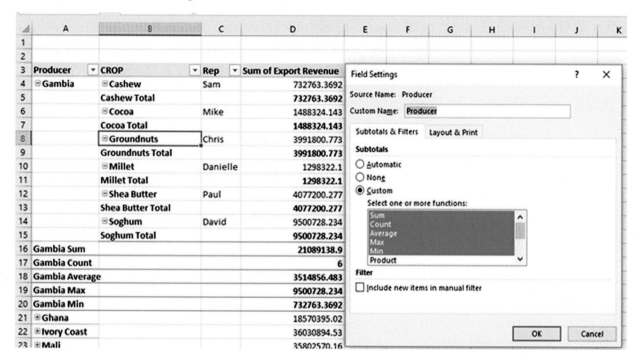

3.6 USING DIFFERENT CALCULATION FOR VALUE FIELDS

The Value **Field Settings** dialog offers different options on the **Summarize Values As** tab and on the **Show Values As** tab

Figure 3.16

CROP	Total Revenue	Average Revenue	# of Orders	% of Total	% of Soghum	Rank	RunTotal	% Run Total
Cashew	$25,393,609	$4,232,268	6	14.86%	73.34%	5	$25,393,609	14.86%
Cocoa	$18,392,465	$3,065,411	6	10.76%	53.12%	6	$43,786,074	25.62%
Groundnuts	$29,763,274	$4,960,546	6	17.41%	85.96%	3	$73,549,348	43.03%
Millet	$28,972,404	$4,828,734	6	16.95%	83.67%	4	$102,521,752	59.98%
Shea Butter	$33,764,891	$5,627,482	6	19.76%	97.51%	2	$136,286,644	79.74%
Soghum	$34,626,007	$5,771,001	6	20.26%	100.00%	1	$170,912,650	100.00%
Grand Total	$170,912,650	$4,747,574	36	100.00%				

3.6.1 SHOWING PERCENTAGE OF TOTAL

Column 5 of Figure 3.16 shows the % of Total. Sorghum with $34.6 million in revenue represent 20.26% of the $170.9 million total revenue. Column 5 uses **% of Column Total** on the **Show Values As** tab. Two other similar options are **% of Row Total** and **% of Grand Total**. Choose one of these based on whether your text fields are going down the report, across the report, or both down and across.

3.6.2 USING %OF TO COMPARE ONE LINE TO ANOTHER LINE

The **% Of** option enables you to compare one item to another item. For example, the current data set shows that Sorghum is the largest selling crop. To set up this calculation, choose **Show Values As**, **% Of**. For the **Base Field**, choose **Crop** and for the **Base Item**, choose **Sorghum**.

3.6.3 SHOWING RANKS

To show up a rank, choose **Value Field Setting**, **Show Values As**, **Rank Largest to Smallest**. You are required to choose a Base Field.

Other calculations that can be achieved from the Value Field include:

- Tracking Running Totals and Percent of Running Total

- Display Change from a Previous Field

- Tracking Percent of Parent Item

- Track Relative Importance with the Index Option

Exercise 3b:

In this exercise, we are going to recreate the pivot table in Figure 3-16. Use the **EnhancePT_A.xlsx** workbook and the **Export** worksheet.

1. **Column 1 (CROP):** Place the **Crop** field in the ROWS area

2. **Column 2 (Total Revenue):** Drag the **Export Revenue** field to the **VALUES** zone

   a. In the pivot table, right-click a cell in the column you just created (the Sum of Export Revenue column) and select "**Value Field Settings**" from the context menu.

   b. In the **Custom Name** text box, type "**Total Revenue**". This replaces the "**Sum of Revenue**" header name. See below.

   c. Click the Number Format tab, and select "Currency". Set the decimal places to zero

Figure 3.17

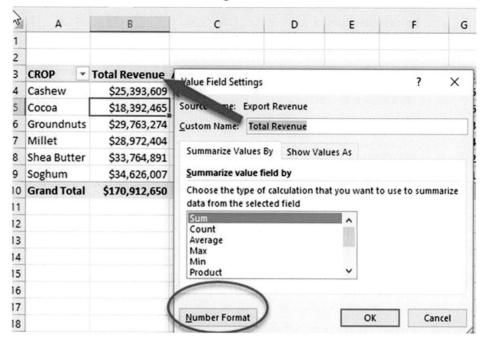

3. **Column 3 (Average Revenue):** Drag the **Export Revenue** field to the **VALUES** zone. Repeat **step 2a**, **step 2b**, and **step 2c** above. In step 2b, in the **Custom Name** text box, type "**Average Revenue**".

    a. Select "**Average**" in the "**Summarize value field by**" list

4. **Column 4 (# of Orders):** Drag the **Export Revenue** field to the **VALUES** zone

    a. Repeat **step 2a** and **step 2b** above. Use "**# of Orders**" for column name, and select the "**Count**" aggregate function

5. **Column 5 (% of Total).** This should be called **% of Column Total.** Drag the **Export Revenue** field to the **VALUES** zone

    a. **Repeat step 2a and step 2b. Use the appropriate name.**

    b. **In the same dialog box, select the "Show Value As" tab**

    c. **In the "Show Value As" dropdown, select "% of Column Total"**

This option calculates each cell value as a ratio of the total in that column. For example, the **Cashew** market's revenue of $25.4 is about 15% of the total revenue. See below

Figure 3.18

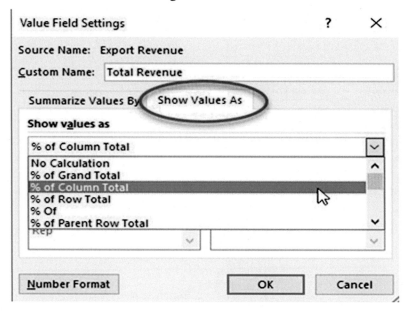

6. **Sorghum has the highest revenue, so we can compare each crop's revenue to that of Sorghum.**

Column 6 (**% Of Sorghum**): Drag the **Export Revenue** field to the VALUES zone

  a. Repeat steps 5a, 5b, and 5c, using the highlighted image below as guide

Figure 3.19

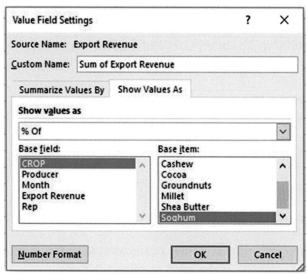

As further exercise for you, complete the pivot table for columns 7 (Rank), column 8 (RunTotal), column 9 (% RunTotal) and column 10 (ChgFromPrevious)

4. GROUPING, SORTING, AND FILTERING PIVOT DATA

In this section of the book, we look at pivot table grouping, sorting, filtering, data visualization, and pivot table options.

4.1 GROUPING PIVOT FIELDS

Transactional data is typically stored with transactional dates. You commonly want to report this data by month, quarter, or year. The **Group** option provides a way to consolidate transactional dates (individual days) into a larger group such as month or quarter. Then you can summarize the data in those groups just as you would with any other field in the pivot table.

4.1.1 GROUPING DATE FIELDS

Figure 4.1 shows part of a pivot report by date. The report spans more columns than shown, which represent the number of rows in the original data set.

Figure 4.1

	A	B	C	D	E	F	G
1							
2							
3	Total Revenue	Date					
4	CROP	27/10/2017	28/10/2017	29/10/2017	1/11/2017	2/11/2017	3/11/2017
5	Cashew	$0	$9,250,231	$0	$0	$0	$0
6	Cocoa	$3,928,020	$0	$0	$0	$0	$0
7	Groundnuts	$0	$0	$0	$0	$0	$839,947
8	Millet	$0	$0	$0	$1,424,883	$0	$0
9	Shea Butter	$0	$0	$1,439,790	$0	$0	$0
10	Soghum	$0	$0	$0	$0	$1,687,525	$0
11	Grand Total	$3,928,020	$9,250,231	$1,439,790	$1,424,883	$1,687,525	$839,947

Create this pivot table in the Grouping.xlsx workbook. Use the Export Crop worksheet. Use the Crop field in the Rows zone. Use Revenue field in the Values zone and the Date field in the Column zone. Right-click one of the Date columns select "Ungroup". To replace null values with zeros (as in the figure above) see section 3.1.3

To group date fields:

- Select any date heading, such as **27/10/2017** in Figure 4.1

- Select **Analysis, Group Field**

The above two steps are not necessary if your report is already grouped by month

By default, the **Months** option is selected. You have choices to group by **Seconds, Minutes, Hours, days, Months, Quarters,** and **Years**. It is advisable to select more than one field in the Grouping dialog.

Figure 4.2

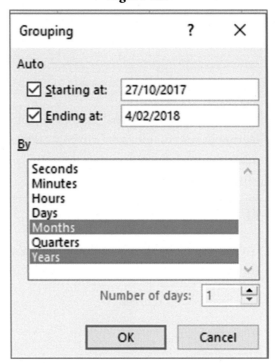

- Select Month and Years as show in Figure 4.2.

Figure 4.3

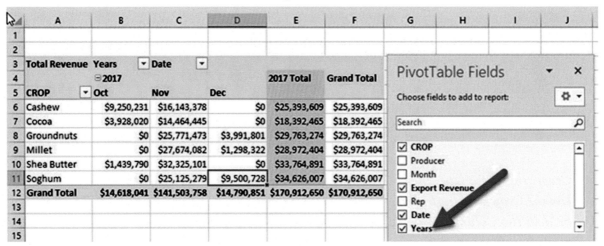

Notice that a **Years** field has been added to the Field List (Figure 4.3). The data source, however, does not include any Years field. The Year field is only part of the pivot cache in memory.

> *Note: To help Excel group data correctly by month, it is important to include years so that Excel does not group months data across different years. In the absence of the years field when grouping by month, Excel will wrongly aggregate January 2016 data with January 2017 data. If this is not intended the months must be qualified by year as we have done in the above example.*

Figure 4.4

	A	B	C	D
1				
2				
3	**Total Revenue**	**Years**		
4	**Month**	**2017**	**2018**	**Grand Total**
5	January	$18,392,465	$14,464,445	$32,856,911
6	February	$25,393,609	$16,143,378	$41,536,986
7	March	$27,674,082	$28,845,843	$56,519,925
8	April	$25,125,279	$42,439,210	$67,564,489
9	Mar	$33,764,891	$32,325,101	$66,089,993
10	Apr	$25,771,473	$32,915,128	$58,686,601
11	**Grand Total**	**$156,121,799**	**$167,133,106**	**$323,254,906**

By now you should be able to produce the above pivot table

Examine the pivot table shown in Figure 4.4. The table has a date field that has been grouped by month and year. The sales for January 2017 is **$18.4m**. However, if you choose to group the dates field only by month, Excel would roll up January 2017 and January 2018 and report as January data.

4.1.2 GROUPING DATE FIELDS BY WEEK

It is also possible to group date by weekly and biweekly basis:

- Determine which day is your first day of the week (usually Sunday)

- Select any date heading in the pivot table. Then select Analyse → Group Field

- In the Grouping dialog, clear all the By options and select only the Days option.

- To produce a report by weeks, increase the number of days in the spin button from 1 to 7

- Set up the Starting At date.

Figure 4.5 shows the setting in the Grouping dialog and the resulting report

Figure 4.5

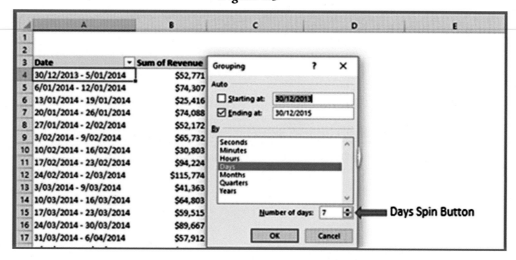

4.1.3 UNGROUPING YOUR DATA

After you have established groups, you can undo the groups by using the **Ungroup** icon on the **Analysis** tab. To undo a group, select one of the grouped cells and then click the **Ungroup** icon on the Analyse tab.

Exercise 4a:

Using the "**Export Crops**" worksheet in the **SortFilterGroup.xlsx**, create a report that groups the CROP field as follows:

- **Cash Crop:** Cocoa, Coffee, Sorghum, Shea Butter

- **Local Crop:** Cashew, Millet, Groundnuts

- **Fruit:** Pineapple, Banana, Orange, Pawpaw, Pear

First, build a report showing sales by crop as shown in Figure 4.6. Use the Outline Layout

Figure 4.6

	A	B
1		
2		
3	Row Labels ⌄	Sum of Sales
4	Banana	2241228.339
5	Cashew	9250230.791
6	Cocoa	3928020.275
7	Coffee	839946.6159
8	Millet	1424882.723
9	Orange	3503523.547
10	Pawpaw	8952813.063
11	Pear	8935641.546
12	Pinaple	3977295.803
13	Shea Butter	1439789.97
14	Soghum	1687524.642
15	Grand Total	46180897.32

- Highlight the four crops that will make up the Cash Crop group.

- From the Analysis tab, click Group Selection. Excel adds a new field called CROP2. The four selected crops are arbitrarily rolled up to a new group called Group1.

Figure 4.7

	A	B	C
1			
2			
3	CROP2 ▾	CROP ▾	Sum of Sales
4	⊟ Banana	Banana	2241228.339
5	**Banana Total**		**2241228.339**
6	⊟ Cashew	Cashew	9250230.791
7	**Cashew Total**		**9250230.791**
8	⊟ Group1	Cocoa	3928020.275
9		Coffee	839946.6159
10		Shea Butter	1439789.97
11		Soghum	1687524.642
12	**Group1 Total**		**7895281.503**
13	⊟ Millet	Millet	1424882.723
14	**Millet Total**		**1424882.723**
15	⊟ Orange	Orange	3503523.547
16	**Orange Total**		**3503523.547**
17	⊟ Pawpaw	Pawpaw	8952813.063
18	**Pawpaw Total**		**8952813.063**
19	⊟ Pear	Pear	8935641.546
20	**Pear Total**		**8935641.546**
21	⊟ Pineapple	Pineapple	3977295.803
22	**Pineapple Total**		**3977295.803**
23	**Grand Total**		**46180897.32**

- Select the crops that make up the Local Crop group.

- Click Group Selection to group the crops in the Local Crops group.

- Select the crops that make up the Fruit group

- Click Group Selection to group the crops for the Fruit group

- Select the "Group1" text and type "Cash Crop" to replace the arbitrary name of Group1 (see Figure 4.8).

- Replace Group2 and Group3 with the appropriate group names

Figure 4.8

	A	B	C
1			
2			
3	CROP2	CROP	Sum of Sales
4	⊟ Group3	Banana	2241228.339
5		Orange	3503523.547
6		Pawpaw	8952813.063
7		Pear	8935641.546
8		Pineapple	3977295.803
9	Group3 Total		27610502.3
10	⊟ Group2	Cashew	9250230.791
11		Millet	1424882.723
12	Group2 Total		10675113.51
13	⊟ Group1	Cocoa	3928020.275
14		Coffee	839946.6159
15		Shea Butter	1439789.97
16		Soghum	1687524.642
17	Group1 Total		7895281.503
18	Grand Total		46180897.32

Figure 4.9

	A	B	C
	CROP2	CROP	Sum of Sales
	⊟ Fruit	Banana	2241228.339
		Orange	3503523.547
		Pawpaw	8952813.063
		Pear	8935641.546
		Pineapple	3977295.803
	Fruit Total		27610502.3
0	⊟ Local Crop	Cashew	9250230.791
1		Millet	1424882.723
2	Local Crop Total		10675113.51
3	⊟ Cash Crop	Cocoa	3928020.275
4		Coffee	839946.6159
5		Shea Butter	1439789.97
6		Soghum	1687524.642
7	Cash Crop Total		7895281.503
8	Grand Total		46180897.32

Figure 4.9 is the final report.

Notice that you can easily compare the sales for the different categories of crops by creating a pivot table for only CROP2 (which contains the categories) as shown in Figure 4.10a

Figure 4.10A

CROP2	Sum of Sales
Fruit	$27,610,502
Local Crop	$10,675,114
Cash Crop	$7,895,282
Grand Total	$46,180,897

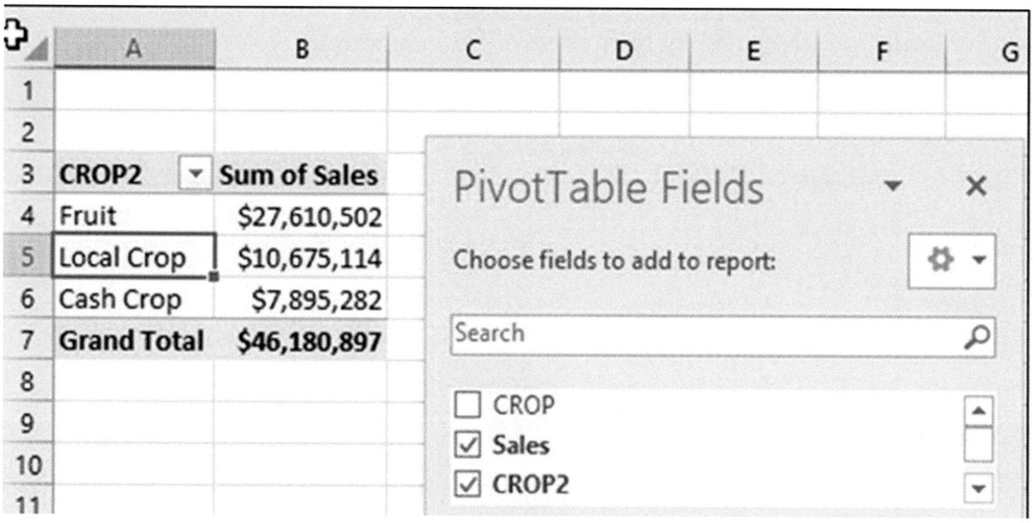

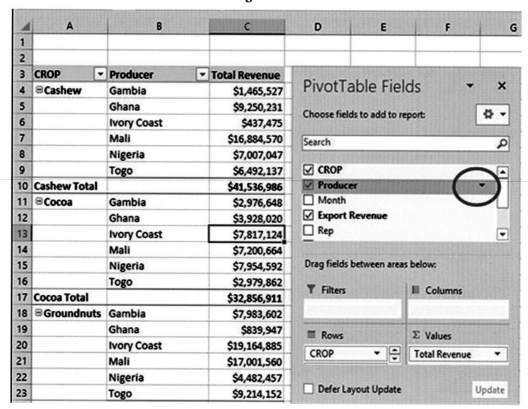

4.2 THE PIVOTTABLE FIELDS LIST

In Figure 4.10 (a Tabular layout), you can use the **Crop** dropdown and the **Producer** dropdown to sort and filter the pivot table report. When you hover over the fields in the PivotTable Fields list, you get a dropdown (red box) list which you can use to filter the report. See the **Producer** dropdown in Figure 4-10

Figure 4.10

CROP	Producer	Total Revenue
Cashew	Gambia	$1,465,527
	Ghana	$9,250,231
	Ivory Coast	$437,475
	Mali	$16,884,570
	Nigeria	$7,007,047
	Togo	$6,492,137
Cashew Total		$41,536,986
Cocoa	Gambia	$2,976,648
	Ghana	$3,928,020
	Ivory Coast	$7,817,124
	Mali	$7,200,664
	Nigeria	$7,954,592
	Togo	$2,979,862
Cocoa Total		$32,856,911
Groundnuts	Gambia	$7,983,602
	Ghana	$839,947
	Ivory Coast	$19,164,885
	Mali	$17,001,560
	Nigeria	$4,482,457
	Togo	$9,214,152

4.2.1 USING THE AREAS SECTION DROP-DOWNS

As shown in Figure 4.11, every field in the Area section has a visible dropdown arrow. When you select the dropdown arrow, you see four categories of choices. These settings are used to rearrange fields in the pivot table such as relative positions of fields in the pivot table column section as well as moving fields to different zones. The "**Field Settings**" category has additional settings. Moreover, the Field Settings category for Rows and Columns zones are different from those of the Values zone. For example, only the Values zone has the "**Show Values As**" choices

Figure 4.11

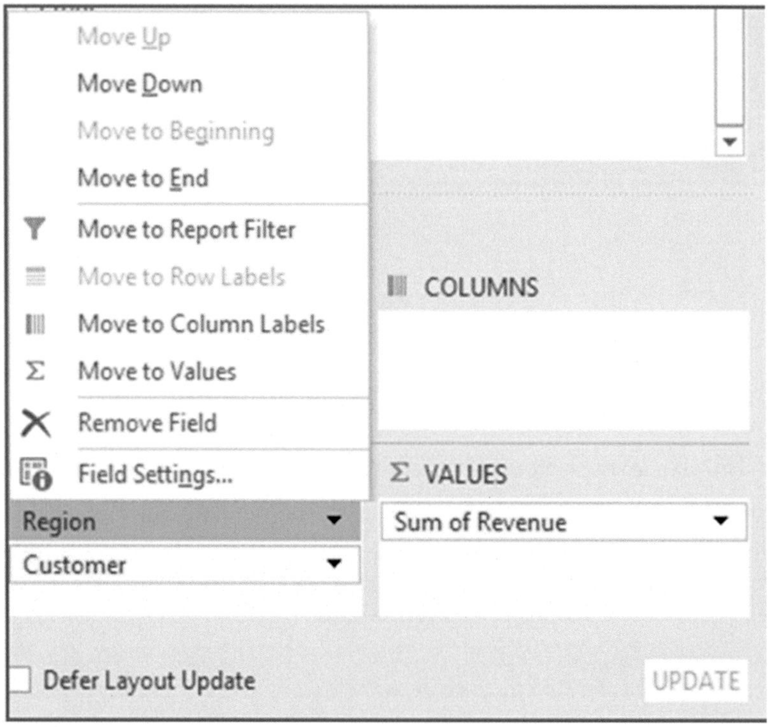

4.3 SORTING IN A PIVOT TABLE

Items in the row area and column area of the pivot table are sorted in ascending order by any custom list first. This allows weekdays and month names to sort into Monday, Tuesday, Wednesday... instead of alphabetical order of Friday, Monday, Saturday, Wednesday... If the items do not appear in a custom list, they will be sorted in ascending order. In some situations, you want the customer with the largest revenue (say) to appear at the top of the list. When you sort in ascending order using a pivot table, you are setting up a rule that controls how that field is sorted, even after new fields are added to the pivot table.

Note: The custom list is defined in the Advanced section of the Excel Options

4.3.1 USING A MANUAL SORT SEQUENCE

You can manually drag and drop the column heading to a new location. Select a column heading. Hover over the edge of the cell selection rectangle until the mouse pointer changes to a four-headed arrow. Drag the cell to a new location, as shown in Figure 4.12. When you release the mouse, all the value settings move to the new column.

Figure 4.12

	A	B	C	D	E	F
1	Sum of Revenue	Product ▾			D2:D5	
2	Date ▾	Doodads	Gadget	Gizmo	Widget	Grand Total
3	⊞2014	$65,216	$1,144,099	$1,152,075	$1,046,163	$3,407,553
4	⊞2015	$8,343	$1,196,997	$1,240,945	$853,974	$3,300,259
5	Grand Total	$73,559	$2,341,096	$2,393,020	$1,900,137	$6,707,812

4.4 A LOOK AT PIVOT TABLE FILTERS

There are many ways to provide filtering in your pivot table. Figure 4.13 shows some of the ways to filter a pivot table report. Each of these methods is discussed.

Figure 4.13

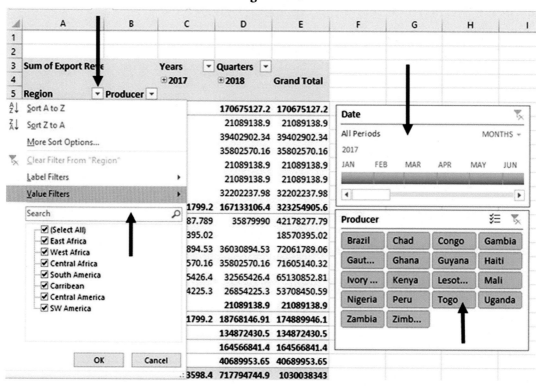

◊   The Timeline filter

◊   The Slicer filters

◊   Dropdowns such as Page Filter and Column Filter dropdowns

◊   The check box filters for each pivot item

◊   A Search box filter

◊   A fly-out menu with **Label Filters**

◊   Some field types also provide **Value Filters** fly-out menu, including the **Top 10** filters, which can do **Top 10, Bottom 5**, **Bottom 3 %**, **Top $8Million** etc.

◊ Depending on the field type, you might see a **Date** filters fly-out menu, with 37 virtual filters such as **Next Month, Last Year, and Year to Date.**

4.5 USING FILTERS FOR ROW AND COLUMN FIELDS

Fields in row and column area of a pivot table provide a dropdown with filtering choices on the header cell for that field. In Figure 4.13, **Regions** dropdown appears at the top, as well as the **Producer** dropdown. If you have multiple row fields, it is just as easy to sort using the invisible dropdown that appear when you hover a field in the top of the PivotTable Field list.

4.5.1 FILTERING USING THE CHECK BOXES

The check box filter provides an easy way to hide some items. For example, you can open the **Product** dropdown and uncheck the product you want to hide

4.5.2 FILTERING USING THE SEARCH BOX

You can use the search box to filter large amount of data. In Figure 4.14, the database includes South American, West African, and Caribbean countries. If you want to narrow the list to African and Caribbean, follow these steps:

1. Open the **Region** dropdown

2. Type "**Africa**" in the search box (Figure 4.14)

3. By default, **Select All Search Result** is selected. Click **OK**

4. Open the **Region** dropdown again

5. Type "**Caribbean**" in the search box

6. Choose **Add Current Selection to Filter** as shown in Figure 4.15 Click OK

Figure 4.14

You now have all regions with either **Africa** or **Caribbean** in the name

Figure 4.15

4.5.3   FILTERING USING THE LABEL FILTERS

Text fields offer fly-out menu called **Label Filters**. To filter out all the Regions, hover the cursor over **Region** field in the Pivot Table Fields list. Click the dropdown next to the field to get the "**Label Filter**" option. You get a pop up dialog box where you can select "**Does Not Contain**" filter (see Figure 4.16). In the next dialog, you can specify that you want regions that do not contain **Africa** (see Figure 4.17).

Figure 4.16

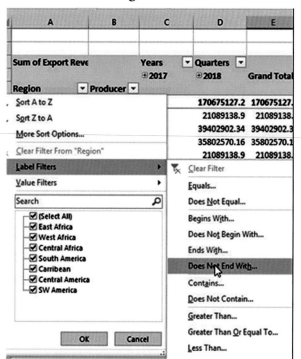

To remove the filter, click on the same dropdown attached to the filtered field and select "**Clear Filter from Customer**". To help you see at a glance which fields are filtered, Excel places the filter icon beside each field that is participating in a filtered report

Figure 4.17

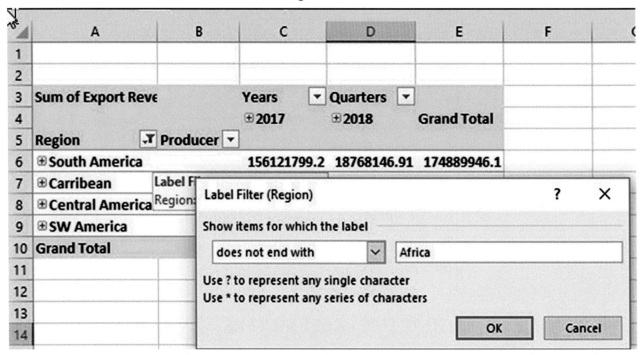

4.5.4 VALUE COLUMN CAN FILTERING LABEL COLUMNS

The Values Filter fly-out menu enables you to filter the Region based on information in the Values columns. For example, to filter for region who had between $15m and $35m of revenue. You can use the Region heading dropdown to control this:

1. Open **Region** dropdown

2. Choose **Value Filters**

3. Choose the "**Between**" option (see Figure 4.18)

4. Type the value **15000000** and **35000000,** as shown in Figure 4.19

Figure 4.18

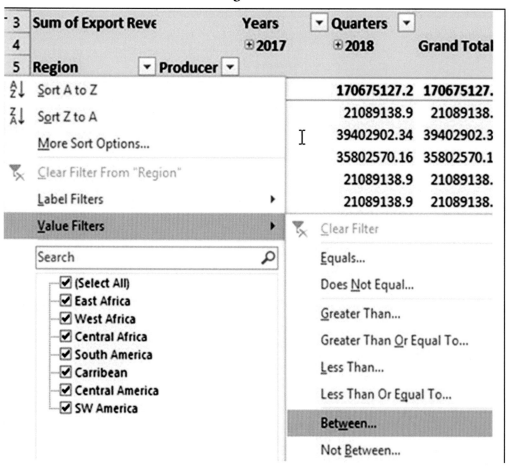

Figure 4.19

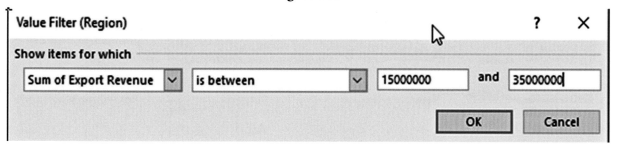

4.5.5 CREATING A TOP-FIVE REPORT USING THE TOP 10 FILTERS

You can use the **Top 10 Filter** to filter your data. "**Top 10**" is a generic name given to this feature. To apply the **Top 10 Filter**:

1. Activate the **Region** dropdown. Choose **Value Filter Top 10**

2. Choose **Top** (default)

3. You can ask for any number of regions: 10, 5, 7, 12. Fill the number in the second fields. For example, to ask for top 10 regions with respect to revenue, you will enter **10** in the **Top 10 Filter** dialog

4. The third dropdown on the dialog offers **Items, Percent**, and **Sum**. You could ask for the top ten items, or the top **80 %** of revenue. You could ask for enough regions to reach a sum of $55 million (see Figure 4.20)

Figure 4.20

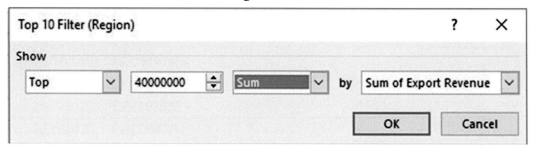

4.5.6 FILTERING USING THE DATE FILTERS IN THE LABEL DROP-DOWN

If your filter is based on a Date field, Excel replaces the Label Filter fly-out with a Date Filter fly-out. These filters offer many virtual filters, such **as Next Week, This Month, Last Quarter**, and so on (see Figure 4.21).

Figure 4.21

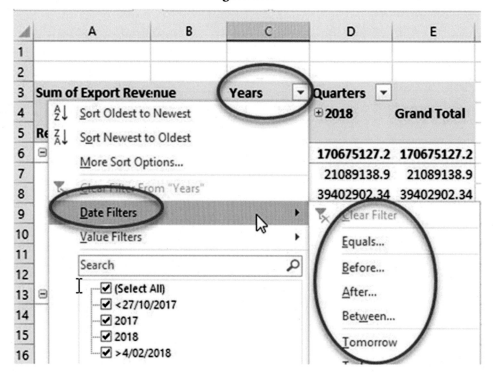

You can pivot a list of projects by due date. Then if you filter the pivot table report with the "**Next Week**" option, you get all the project tasks that are due in the next week. When you open the workbook on another day, the report recalculates and produces all project tasks that are due next week from the time the report was opened.

4.6 FILTERING USING THE FILTERS AREA

Note: If you want to follow the discussion in your pivot table, use the Grouping.xlsm workbook

To set up filtered report, drag **Export Revenue** to the **Value** drop zone and then drag as many fields as desired to the filtered drop zone, as shown in Figure 4.22. If you add many fields in the **Filters** area, you can divide the filter fields into groups. Click **Analyse → Options** tab. On the **Layout & Format** tab of the **PivotTable Options** dialog, change the **Report Filter Fields Per Column** from 0 to a positive number. Figure 4.22 has two fields per column

Figure 4.22

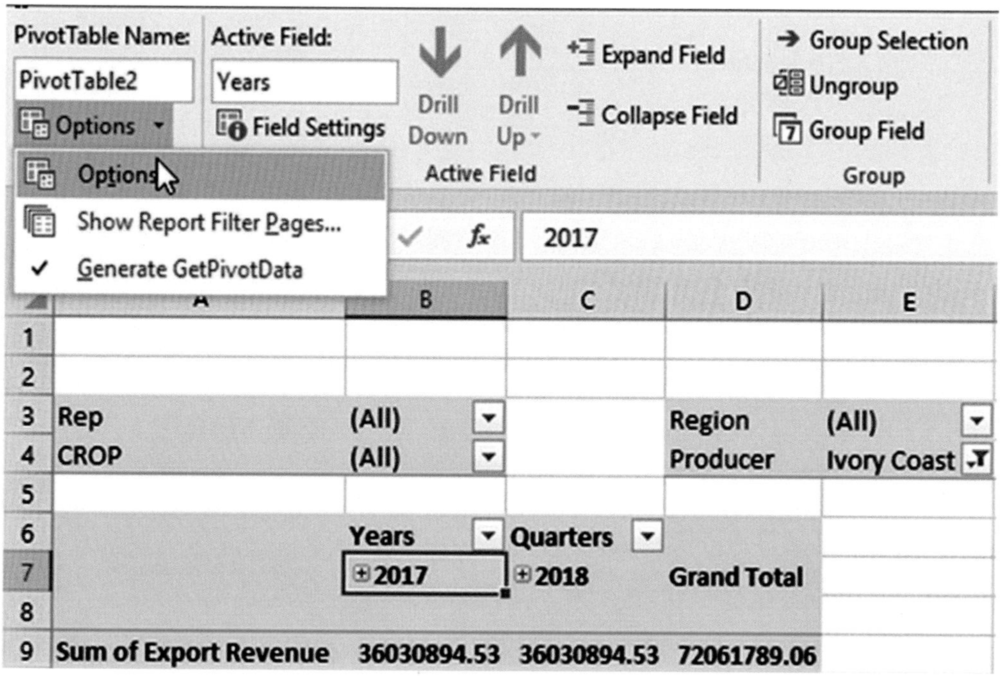

4.6.1 CHOOSING ONE ITEM FROM A FILTER

To filter the pivot table, click any dropdown in the **Filters** area of the pivot table. The dropdown always starts with **(All),** but then lists the complete unique set of items available in that field

4.6.2 CHOOSING MULTIPLE ITEMS FROM A REPORT FILTER

At the bottom of the filter dropdown is a checkbox labelled **Select Multiple Items**. If you select this box, Excel adds a checkbox next to each item in the dropdown. This enables you to check multiple items from the list. In Figure 4.23, the pivot table is filtered to show revenue **for Cocoa** and **Millet**.

Figure 4.23

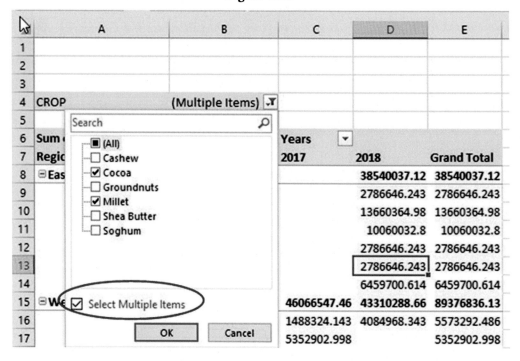

4.6.3 DISTRIBUTING A PIVOT TABLE REPORT FOR EACH ITEM IN A FILTER

You can share your pivot table reports with colleagues so that each person can receive only the data he/she is supposed to receive.

To demonstrate, follow these steps. We will create a report that will be distribute to each Rep, and each Rep will receive only the data pertaining to him/her:

Use the **Export Crops** worksheet in the **Grouping.xlsx** workbook to create a pivot table report as follows:

Exercise 4b:

COLUMNS Zone: **Years**

ROWS Zone: **Region, Producer**

VALUES Zone: **Export Revenue**

FILTER Zone: **Rep**

Layout: **Outline Form**

1. Ensure that "**ALL**" is selected in the **Rep** filter.

2. Select one cell in the pivot table.

3. In the **PivotTable** group, choose **Analyse, Options Show Report Filter Pages**…

4. In the **Show Report Filter Pages** dialog, you see a list of all the fields in the report filter area. Because this pivot table only has the **Rep** filter field, this is the only choice (see Figure 4.24)

Figure 4.24

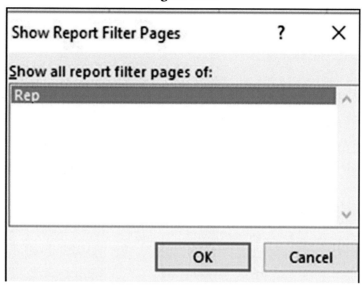

Excel inserts a new worksheet data for every rep in the Rep (filter) field as shown in Figure4-24a

Figure 4.24A

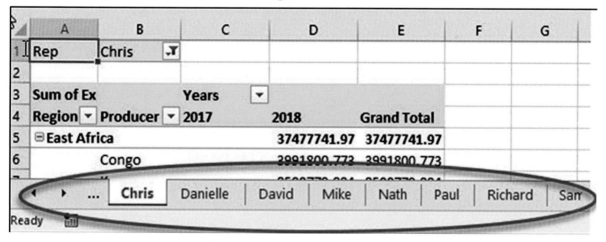

4.7 FILTERING USING SLICERS AND TIMELINES

To add slicers:

1. Choose **Analyse, Insert Slicers**. Excel displays the Insert Slicers dialog

2. Choose all the fields for which you want to create graphical filters as shown in Figure 4.25

Figure 4.25

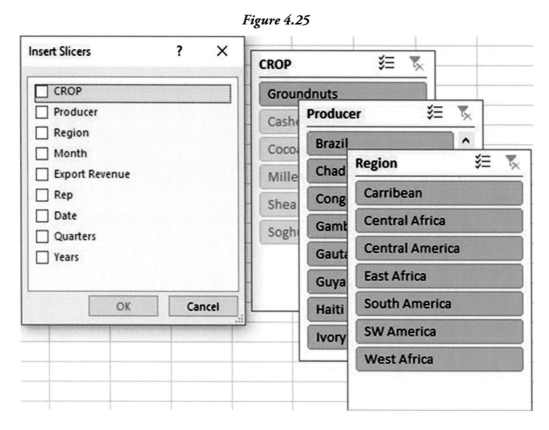

You can add more columns to a slicer by using the **Columns Spin** button. See Figure 4-26.

Note: The slicer Columns spin button is displayed only when the slicer is selected

Figure 4.26

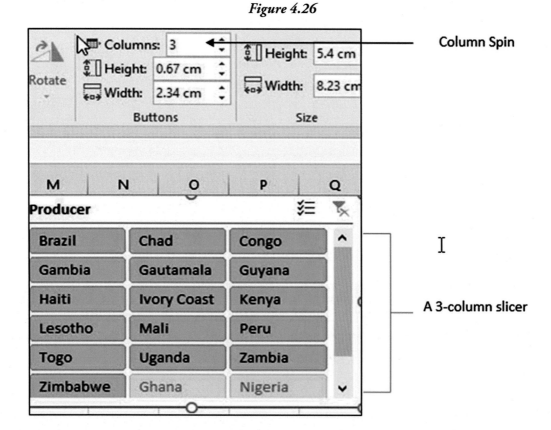

4.7.1 FILTERING BY DATE

You can filter your data by using dates.

To create Timeline filter:

Select one cell in the pivot table and choose **Insert Timeline** from the **Analyse** tab. Timelines can only apply to date fields. See Figure 4-27

Figure 4.27

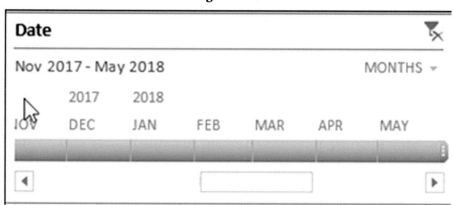

You can link multiple pivot tables to a single set of slicers

Figure 4.28

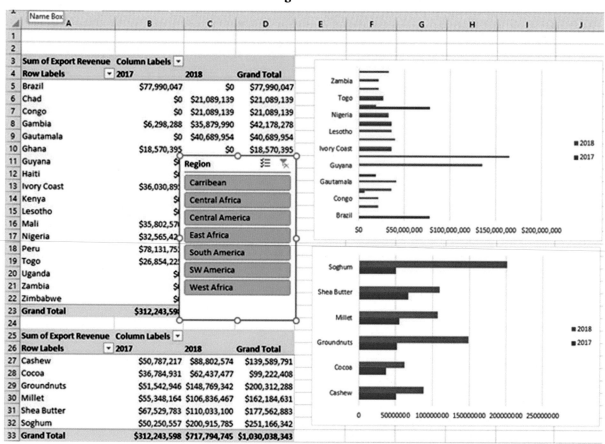

In Figure 4-28, the **Region** slicer is driving four elements: The two pivot tables and the two pivot charts.

1. Create the first pivot table:

    a. **Columns Zone: Years**

    b. **Rows Zone: Producer**

    c. **Values Zone: Revenue**

2. Select a cell in the pivot table. Press **Ctrl + A** to select the entire pivot table, then (**Ctrl+C**) to copy

3. Paste to a blank area of the worksheet. The two pivot tables share the same pivot cache. For one slicer to run multiple pivot table, they must share the same pivot cache

4. Change the fields in the second pivot table to show some other interesting analysis. For example, use the **Crops** in the **Rows** area and remove the existing field

5. Create two separate bar charts, one for each pivot tables

6. Select a cell in the first pivot table. Choose **Insert Slicers**. Create a slicer for the **Region** field

7. Click the slicer to select it.

8. Select the **Slicer Tool, Options** tab and choose **Report Connection**. Excel displays **the Report Connection (Region)** dialog. Initially, only the first pivot table is selected

9. Select the other pivot tables in the dialog and click **OK**

5. EXTEND COLUMNS AND ROWS WITH CALCULATIONS

Note: All pivot tables in this section are based on the Calculations.xlsx workbook

Excel provides a way to perform calculations within a pivot table through calculated fields and calculated items.

5.1 CALCULATED FIELDS AND CALCULATED ITEMS

A *calculated field* (or **calculated column**) is a data field you create by executing a calculation that uses existing fields in the pivot table. A calculated field is a column/field stored in the data model that can extend the content of a table. They are like new columns defined with formulas in an Excel table. A calculated column is just like any other column in a pivot table. It can be used in rows, columns, filters, or values of a pivot table. The expression defined for a calculated column operates in the context of the current row of the table that it belongs to. Any reference to a column returns the value of that column in the current row. You cannot access directly the values of other rows. The expression of the calculated column is evaluated for each row, and its result is stored in the table as if it were a column retrieved from the database. A *calculated item* is a data item you create by executing a calculation against existing items within a data field. A calculated item is an expression that uses the same syntax as a calculated column; the difference is in the context of evaluation. A calculated item is evaluated in the context of the cell of the pivot table; that is, filter context applies. The value of this cell is determined by the filters applied by the user selections, whereas a calculated column is computed at the row level of the power pivot table, that is row context. The cell context depends on the user selection on the PivotTable. When you use **SUM(SalesAmount)** in a calculated item, you mean the sum of all the rows that are aggregated under the PivotTable cell (filters apply), whereas when you use **Sales[SalesAmount]** in a calculated column, you mean the value of **SalesAmount** in *this row*.

Figure 5.1

	A	B	C	D	E	F
2						
3	°- ▼	Sales_Amount	Contracted Hours	Dollar Per Hour		
4	BUFFALO	$450,478.27	$6,864.00	$65.63		
5	CALIFORNIA	$2,254,735.38	$33,014.00	$68.30		
6	CANADA	$776,245.27	$12,103.00	$64.14		
7	CHARLOTTE	$890,522.49	$14,525.00	$61.31		
8	DALLAS	$467,089.47	$6,393.00	$73.06		
9	DENVER	$645,583.29	$8,641.00	$74.71		
10	FLORIDA	$1,450,392.00	$22,640.00	$64.06		
11	KANSASCITY	$574,898.97	$8,547.00	$67.26		
12	MICHIGAN	$678,704.95	$10,744.00	$63.17		
13	NEWORLEANS	$333,453.65	$5,057.00	$65.94		
14	NEWYORK	$873,580.91	$14,213.00	$61.46	I	
15	PHOENIX	$570,255.09	$10,167.00	$56.09		
16	SEATTLE	$179,827.21	$2,889.00	$62.25		
17	TULSA	$628,404.83	$9,583.00	$65.57		
18	Grand Total	$10,774,171.78	$165,380.00	$65.15		
19						
20						
21				Calculated Field: Sales Amount/Contracted Hours		

Figure 5.1 is an example of a calculated field that shows the average dollar per hour for each market

5.2 CREATING A CALCULATED FIELD

To create the **Calculated Field** shown in Figure 5.1, first create a pivot table as shown in Figure 5.2

Figure 5.2

	A	B	C
2			
3	*-	Sales_Amount	Contracted Hours
4	BUFFALO	$450,478.27	$6,864.00
5	CALIFORNIA	$2,254,735.38	$33,014.00
6	CANADA	$776,245.27	$12,103.00
7	CHARLOTTE	$890,522.49	$14,525.00
8	DALLAS	$467,089.47	$6,393.00
9	DENVER	$645,583.29	$8,641.00
10	FLORIDA	$1,450,392.00	$22,640.00
11	KANSASCITY	$574,898.97	$8,547.00
12	MICHIGAN	$678,704.95	$10,744.00
13	NEWORLEANS	$333,453.65	$5,057.00
14	NEWYORK	$873,580.91	$14,213.00
15	PHOENIX	$570,255.09	$10,167.00
16	SEATTLE	$179,827.21	$2,889.00
17	TULSA	$628,404.83	$9,583.00
18	Grand Total	$10,774,171.78	$165,380.00

- Select **Pivot Table Tools → Analyse → Calculations Fields, Items, & Sets → Calculated Field**. The **Insert Calculated Field** dialog appears as shown in Figure 5.3.

Figure 5.3

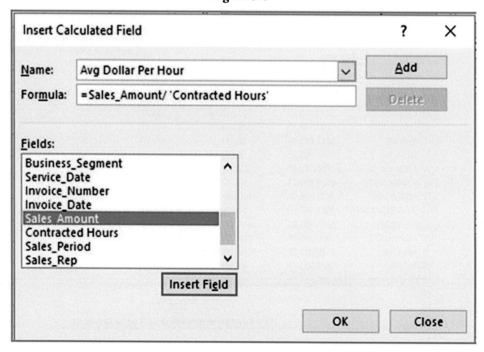

- Type the name of the calculated field in the Name textbox. In this case, enter "Avg Dollar Per Hour"

- In the Formula text box, enter =Sales_Amount/Contracted Hour (see Figure 5.3). You can also double-click the item (e.g. Sales_Amount) in the Fields list box to populate the Formula textbox

- When the formula is entered, click Add, then OK.

A new field called **Sum of Avg. Dollar Per Hour** is added to the pivot table and to the PivotTable Fields list.

Exercises 5a:

Use the Calculations.xlsx workbook (Case Study worksheet)

Create a pivot table to provide the following analyses

◊   Total revenue forecast by market

◊   Total percent growth over last year

◊   Total contribution margin by market

Start by building the initial pivot table, shown in Figure 5.4

Figure 5.4

Row Labels	Sum of Revenue Last Year	Sum of Forecast Next Year	Sum of Percent Growth
BUFFALO	450478.27	411245.937	-8.71%
CALIFORNIA	2254735.38	2423007	7.46%
CANADA	776245.27	746383.9429	-3.85%
CHARLOTTE	890522.49	965360.5587	8.40%
DALLAS	467089.47	510635.3401	9.32%
DENVER	645583.29	722694.9512	11.94%
FLORIDA	1450392	1421506.578	-1.99%
KANSASCITY	574898.97	607226.3176	5.62%
MICHIGAN	678704.95	870446.7319	28.25%
NEWORLEANS	333453.65	366173.5523	9.81%
NEWYORK	873580.91	953009.8559	9.09%
PHOENIX	570255.09	746721.3941	30.95%
SEATTLE	179827.21	214620.9621	19.35%
TULSA	628404.83	661726.4452	5.30%
Grand Total	**10774171.78**	**11620759.57**	**7.86%**

The pivot table answers the first requirement: Total revenue forecast by market

The next metric you need is the percent growth over last year. To get this, you need to add a calculated field that uses the following formula:

(Forecast Next Year / Revenue Last Year) - 1

To achieve this, do the following:

1.   Activate the **Insert Calculated Field** dialog and name the new field **Percent Growth** (see Figure 5.5)

Figure 5.5

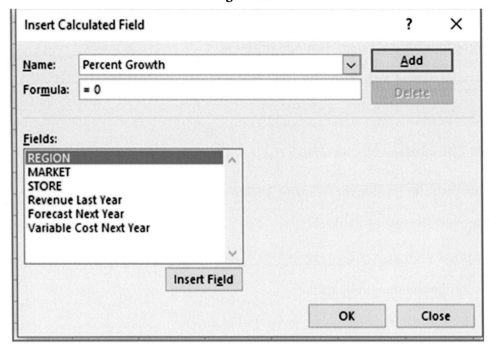

2. In the Formula input box enter the formula: **=(Forecast Next Year /Revenue Last Year) – 1**

3. After you click **Add**, the pivot table is updated with the new calculated field. Apply the **Percent Format** to the new field (see Figure 5.6)

Figure 5.6

Row Labels	Sum of Revenue Last Year	Sum of Forecast Next Year	Sum of Percent Growth	Sum of Contribution Margin
BUFFALO	450478.27	411245.937	-8.71%	($169,546)
CALIFORNIA	2254735.38	2423007	7.46%	$1,152,641
CANADA	776245.27	746383.9429	-3.85%	$118,415
CHARLOTTE	890522.49	965360.5587	8.40%	$360,343
DALLAS	467089.47	510635.3401	9.32%	($908,021)
DENVER	645583.29	722694.9512	11.94%	($697,393)
FLORIDA	1450392	1421506.578	-1.99%	$865,700
KANSASCITY	574898.97	607226.3176	5.62%	($328,773)
MICHIGAN	678704.95	870446.7319	28.25%	($92,813)
NEWORLEANS	333453.65	366173.5523	9.81%	($586,405)
NEWYORK	873580.91	953009.8559	9.09%	$506,335
PHOENIX	570255.09	746721.3941	30.95%	$318,496
SEATTLE	179827.21	214620.9621	19.35%	($163,738)
TULSA	628404.83	661726.4452	5.30%	($1,193,984)
Grand Total	**10774171.78**	**11620759.57**	**7.86%**	**($818,743)**

With the "**Percent Growth Over Last Year**" calculated column in place, you can easily see that three markets need to resubmit their forecasts to reflect positive growth over last year

The last requirement is to find total contribution margin by market. To get this data, you need to add a calculated field using the following formula:

Forecast Next Year + Variable Cost Next Year.

Notice that the "**Variable Cost Next Year**" is not in the pivot table, yet we can still use it to build a calculated field.

To create this field, do the following:

Activate the **Insert Calculated Field** dialog box and name the new field **Contribution Margin**

Enter the formula **Forecast Next Year + Variable Cost Next Year** into the Formula input box

With this, the report is ready, as shown in Figure 5.7

You can rename the column headings

Figure 5.7

Row Labels	Revenue Last Year	Forecast Next Year	Sum of Percent Growth	Sum of Contribution Margin
BUFFALO	$450,478	$411,246	-8.7%	($169,546)
CALIFORNIA	$2,254,735	$2,423,007	7.5%	$1,152,641
CANADA	$776,245	$746,384	-3.8%	$118,415
CHARLOTTE	$890,522	$965,361	8.4%	$360,343
DALLAS	$467,089	$510,635	9.3%	($908,021)
DENVER	$645,583	$722,695	11.9%	($697,393)
FLORIDA	$1,450,392	$1,421,507	-2.0%	$865,700
KANSASCITY	$574,899	$607,226	5.6%	($328,773)
MICHIGAN	$678,705	$870,447	28.3%	($92,813)
NEWORLEANS	$333,454	$366,174	9.8%	($586,405)
NEWYORK	$873,581	$953,010	9.1%	$506,335
PHOENIX	$570,255	$746,721	30.9%	$318,496
SEATTLE	$179,827	$214,621	19.3%	($163,738)
TULSA	$628,405	$661,726	5.3%	($1,193,984)
Grand Total	$10,774,172	$11,620,760	7.9%	($818,743)

5.3 CREATING A CALCULATED ITEM

Note: Use the CalculatedItem worksheet in the Calculate.xlsx workbook. Place the SalesCode in the Rows zone, Product in the Column zone and Tonnage in the Values zone

When you create a calculated item, you are effectively creating an aggregation of your data in memory. Calculated items extend the rows of your data as opposed to calculated columns that extend the columns of the data

Figure 5.8

⊿	A	B	C	D
1				
2				
3	**Sum of Tonnes**	**Column Labels** ⏷		
4	**Row Labels** ⏷	**Cocoa**	**Coffee**	**Grand Total**
5	Cocoa01	29467738.84		29467738.84
6	Cocoa02	73427072.92		73427072.92
7	Cocoa03	5948366.089		5948366.089
8	Cocoa04	5189010.325		5189010.325
9	Cocoa05	69777196.4		69777196.4
10	Cocoa06	16782575.7		16782575.7
11	Cocoa07	7221287.568		7221287.568
12	Cocoa08	84998849.68		84998849.68
13	Cocoa09	87648047.61		87648047.61
14	Coffee01		60219185.27	60219185.27
15	Coffee02		3977354.047	3977354.047
16	Coffee03		94269978.19	94269978.19
17	Coffee04		95954623.4	95954623.4
18	Coffee05		93728634.25	93728634.25
19	Coffee06		74478181.07	74478181.07
20	Coffee07		42959056.19	42959056.19
21	**Grand Total**	380460145.1	465587012.4	846047157.5

The pivot table in Figure 5.8 shows cocoa and coffee production for some West African countries in a specific period. Assume that you want to compare the average cocoa production within this period with the production of coffee

1. Place the cursor on any data in the **SalesCode** field

2. In the Analyse tab in the **PivotTable Tools** group, select **Fields, Items, & Sets** from the **Calculations** group

3. Select **Calculated Item** as shown in Figure 5.9

Figure 5-9

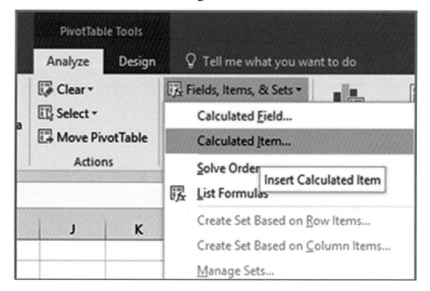

4. Select Calculated Item to open the Insert Calculated Item dialog as shown in Figure 5.10

Figure 5-10

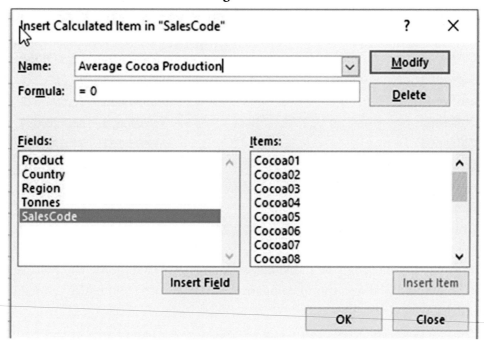

The Items list box is automatically filled with all the items in the SalesCode field.

- Give a name to the calculate item (**Avg. Cocoa Production**)

- In the Formula input box, enter the following formula:

- **Average (Cocoa01, Cocoa02, Cocoa03, Cocoa04, Cocoa05, Cocoa06, Cocoa07, Cocoa08, Cocoa09)**

- Click **OK** to create the new calculated item. Figure 5.11 shows the data item called **Avg. Cocoa Production.**

- Create the second calculated item called **Average Coffee Production**. The two calculated items are shown in Figure 5.11

Figure 5-11

	A	B	C	D
1				
2				
3	**Sum of Tonnes**	**Column Labels**		
4	**Row Labels**	**Cocoa**	**Coffee**	**Grand Total**
5	Cocoa01	29,467,739		29,467,739
6	Cocoa02	73,427,073		73,427,073
7	Cocoa03	5,948,366		5,948,366
8	Cocoa04	5,189,010		5,189,010
9	Cocoa05	69,777,196		69,777,196
10	Cocoa06	16,782,576		16,782,576
11	Cocoa07	7,221,288		7,221,288
12	Cocoa08	84,998,850		84,998,850
13	Cocoa09	87,648,048		87,648,048
14	Coffee01		60,219,185	60,219,185
15	Coffee02		3,977,354	3,977,354
16	Coffee03		94,269,978	94,269,978
17	Coffee04		95,954,623	95,954,623
18	Coffee05		93,728,634	93,728,634
19	Coffee06		74,478,181	74,478,181
20	Coffee07		42,959,056	42,959,056
21	**Average Cocoa Production**	42,273,349	0	42,273,349
22	**Average Coffee Production**	0	66,512,430	66,512,430
23	**Grand Total**	422,733,495	532,099,443	954,832,937

Now you can hide (by filtering) the individual sales periods, leaving only the two calculated items. The final report (Figure 5.12) allows you to compare the average cocoa and coffee productions in tonnes for these West African countries.

Figure 5-12

	A	B	C	D
1				
2				
3	**Sum of Tonnes**	**Column Labels**		
4	**Row Labels**	**Cocoa**	**Coffee**	**Grand Total**
5	**Average Cocoa Production**	42,273,349	0	42,273,349
6	**Average Coffee Production**	0	66,512,430	66,512,430
7	**Grand Total**	42,273,349	66,512,430	108,785,780

5.4 CALCULATIONS LIVE BY RULES

The following sections highlight the rules around calculated items and calculated fields that are likely to cause errors in pivot table calculations.

5.4.1 USING CELL REFERENCES AND NAMED RANGES

When you create calculations in a pivot table, the only data available to you is the data that exists in the pivot cache. Therefore, you cannot go outside the confines of the pivot cache to reference cells or named ranges in the formula. This is generally not a problem because when you start creating a calculation, only the fields that are in the cache are presented to you, see Figure 5-10. Even if you have defined a named range in the pivot table you will not be able to access it

5.4.2 USING WORKSHEET FUNCTIONS

When building calculated fields or calculated items, Excel allows the use of worksheet functions that accept numeric values as arguments and return numeric values as results in calculated fields and calculated items. Examples include **COUNT, AVERAGE, IF, AND, NOT**, and **OR**. Some examples of functions you could not use are **VLOOKUP, INDEX, SUMIF, COUNTIF, LEFT**, and **RIGHT**. These either require cell array references or return textual values as the result.

5.4.3 USING CONSTANTS

You can use any constant in pivot table calculations.

5.4.4 REFERENCING TOTALS AND SUBTOTALS

Calculation formulas cannot reference a pivot table's subtotals or grand totals.

5.4.5 RULES FOR CALCULATED FIELDS

Calculated fields calculations are always performed against the sum of your data. Excel always calculates data fields, subtotals, and grand totals before evaluating your calculated field. This means that your calculated field is always applied to the sum of the underlying data. The following example (Figure 5.13) demonstrates how this can adversely affect your data analysis

Figure 5-13

	A	B	C	D	E
1					
2					
3	**Quarters**	**Product**	**Quantity**	**Cost**	**Quantity * Cost**
4	⊟**Qtr1**	Doodads	1100	$10,984	$12,082,400
5		Gadget	20500	$252,394	$5,174,077,000
6		Gizmo	24200	$311,724	$7,543,720,800
7		Widget	27500	$296,275	$8,147,562,500
8	**Qtr1 Total**		73300	$871,377	$63,871,934,100

The grand total for **Qtr1** ($63,871,934,100) is not correct. This is because the formula (**Quantity * Cost**) was applied to the Qtr1 subtotal which is not the same as summing the individual **Quantity * Cost** for each product. The solution is to eliminate subtotals and grand totals from the pivot report and calculate them manually

So, in the above table, the **Qtr1 Total** (63871934100) was computer as **73300 * 871377**. Clearly this should be the sum of the individual Quantity * Cost for each item. This is because the calculated field was computed against the pivot table data and the computation did not differentiate between grand totals and subtotals and the rest of the data

Exercise 5a:

Open a new workbook and enter the following data in a worksheet:

Figure 5.13A

	A	B	C	D
1	Product	Units	Price	Qtr
2	A	10	22	Q1
3	B	5	30	Q1
4	C	5	44	Q1
5	D	11	54	Q1

Create a pivot table as shown below. Use the Outline report layout:

Figure 5.13B

Create a calculated field called "**Total Cost**" using the formula **Units * Price**. Verify if the grand total is correct. If not explain why. Remove the "**Total Cost**" calculated field from the model.

Expand the data set as shown below and repeat the process

Figure 5.13C

	Product	Units	Price	Qtr
1	Product	Units	Price	Qtr
2	A	10	22	Q1
3	B	5	30	Q1
4	C	5	44	Q1
5	D	11	54	Q1
6	A	45	33	Q2
7	B	32	56	Q2
8	C	12	7	Q2
9	D	34	23	Q2

5.4.6 RULES FOR CALCULATED ITEMS

Calculated items cannot be created in a pivot table that uses averages, standard deviations, or variances. Conversely, you cannot use averages, standard deviations, or variances in a pivot table that contains a calculated item.

Page Fields cannot be used to create a calculated item, nor can you move any calculated item to the report filter area. This means that if you place a field in the Filters area, that field cannot be used as part of a calculated item computation

You cannot add a calculated item to a report that has a grouped field, nor can you group any field in a pivot table that contains a calculated item

When building the calculated item formula, you cannot reference items from a field other than the one you are working with

5.5 MANAGING AND MAINTAINING PIVOT TABLE CALCULATIONS

Sometimes it becomes necessary to keep a pivot table around for a long time. The pivot table will need maintenance as the source data changes

5.5.1 EDITING AND DELETING PIVOT TABLE CALCULATIONS

To edit or delete a calculated field or calculated item:

- Activate the **Insert Calculated Field** or **Insert Calculated Item** dialog

- Select the **Name** dropdown, as demonstrated in Figure 5.14

Figure 5-14

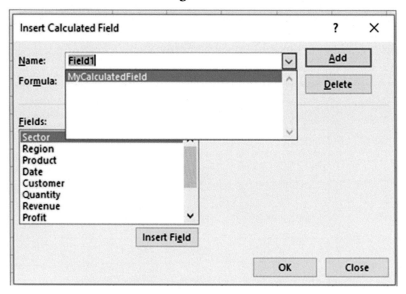

In Figure 5-14, the "**MyCalculatedField**" is an existing calculated field that you want to modify

After you select a calculated field or item, you get the option to delete or modify the calculation.

5.5.2 DOCUMENTING FORMULAS

You can keep track of the list of calculated items and calculated fields in your pivot table

To list a pivot table calculations, simply place the cursor within the pivot table and select **Fields, Items, & Sets** and then select **List Formula**. Excel creates a new worksheet listing the calculated fields and Calculated Items in the current pivot table. Figure 5.15 shows a sample output of the **List Formula** command.

If a value in a Pivot Table cell is affected by two or more calculated items, the value is determined by the last formula in the solve order. To change the solve order for multiple calculated items or fields, on the **Options** tab, in the **Calculation** group, click **Fields, Items, & Sets**, and then click **Solve Order** (see Figure 5.16)

Figure 5.16

	A	B	C	D	E	F
1	*Calculated Field*					
2	**Solve Order**	Field	Formula			
3		1 Avg Dollar Per Hour	=Sales_Amount/'Contracted Hours'			
4		2 Avg Dollar Per Hour	=Sales_Amount/'Contracted Hours'			
5						
6	*Calculated Item*					
7	**Solve Order**	Item	Formula			
8		1 MyCalculatedItem	=AVERAGE(BUFFALO,CALIFORNIA,CANADA)			
9		2 MyCalculatedItem1	=AVERAGE(BUFFALO,CALIFORNIA,CANADA)			
10						
11						
12	*Note:*	When a cell is updated by more than one formula,				
13		the value is set by the formula with the last solve order.				
14						
15		To change the solve order for multiple calculated items or fields,				
16		on the Options tab, in the Calculations group, click Fields, Items, & Sets, and then click Solve Order.				

6. USING PIVOT CHARTS AND OTHER VISUALIZATIONS

It can be hard to see the big picture when you have data in a huge PivotTable or when you have a lot of complex worksheet data that includes text and numbers with column headings.

A PivotChart can help you make sense of this data. While a PivotChart shows data series, categories, and chart axes the same way a standard chart does, it also gives you interactive filtering controls right on the chart so you can quickly analyze a subset of your data.

6.1 CREATING YOUR FIRST PIVOT CHART

To create a pivot chart for the pivot table shown in Figure 6.1:

Figure 6-1

	A	B
1		
2		
3	Row Labels	Sum of Tonnes
4	Brazil	77990046.72
5	Chad	21089138.9
6	Congo	21089138.9
7	Gambia	42178277.79
8	Gautamala	40689953.65
9	Ghana	18570395.02
10	Guyana	134872430.5
11	Haiti	164566841.4
12	Ivory Coast	72061789.06
13	Kenya	39402902.34
14	Lesotho	35802570.16
15	Mali	71605140.32
16	Nigeria	65130852.81
17	Peru	96899899.39
18	Togo	53708450.59
19	Uganda	21089138.9
20	Zambia	21089138.9
21	Zimbabwe	32202237.98
22	**Grand Total**	**1030038343**

- Place the cursor inside the pivot table

- Click **Insert Charts**

- Click **Column** chart icon and select the first 2-D column chart, as demonstrated in Figure 6.2

Figure 6-2

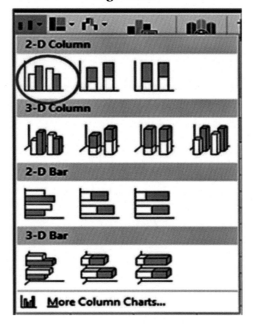

The pivot chart appears on the same data sheet as shown in Figure 6.3. This chart is the visual representation of the pivot table. Because the pivot chart is tied to the underlying pivot table, changes to the pivot table are reflected in the chart. Any filters applied to the pivot table also shows in the pivot chart. This behaviour is the results of the common pivot cache shared by the pivot table and the pivot chart.

Figure 6-3

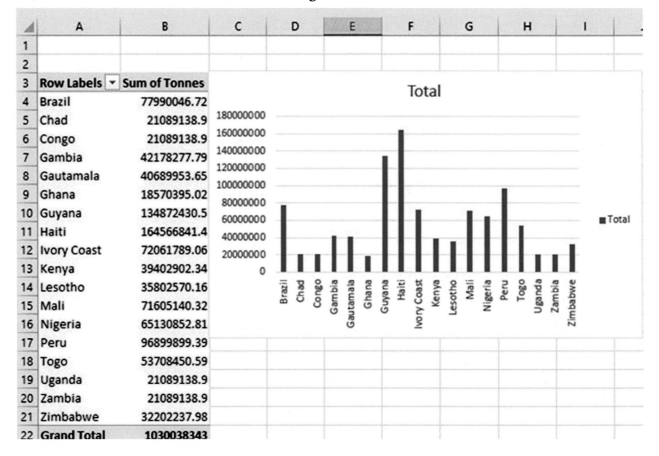

6.2 THINGS TO KNOW ABOUT CHARTS

The following are some titbits for charts

6.2.1   PIVOT TABLE AND PIVOT CHARTS WORK TOGETHER

The primary rule is that the pivot chart is merely an extension of the pivot table. If you refresh, move a field, add a field, remove a field, hide a data item, show data item, or apply a filter, the pivot chart redraws to reflect the changes.

6.2.2   PLACEMENT OF DATA FIELD IN PIVOT TABLE

In a pivot chart, both the x-axis and the y-axis correspond to a specific area in the pivot table:

◊   **Y-axis** – Corresponds to the column area in the pivot table and make up the y-axis of the pivot chart

◊   **X-axis** – Corresponds to the row area in the pivot table and make up the x-axis of the pivot chart. See Figure 6.4

Figure 6-4

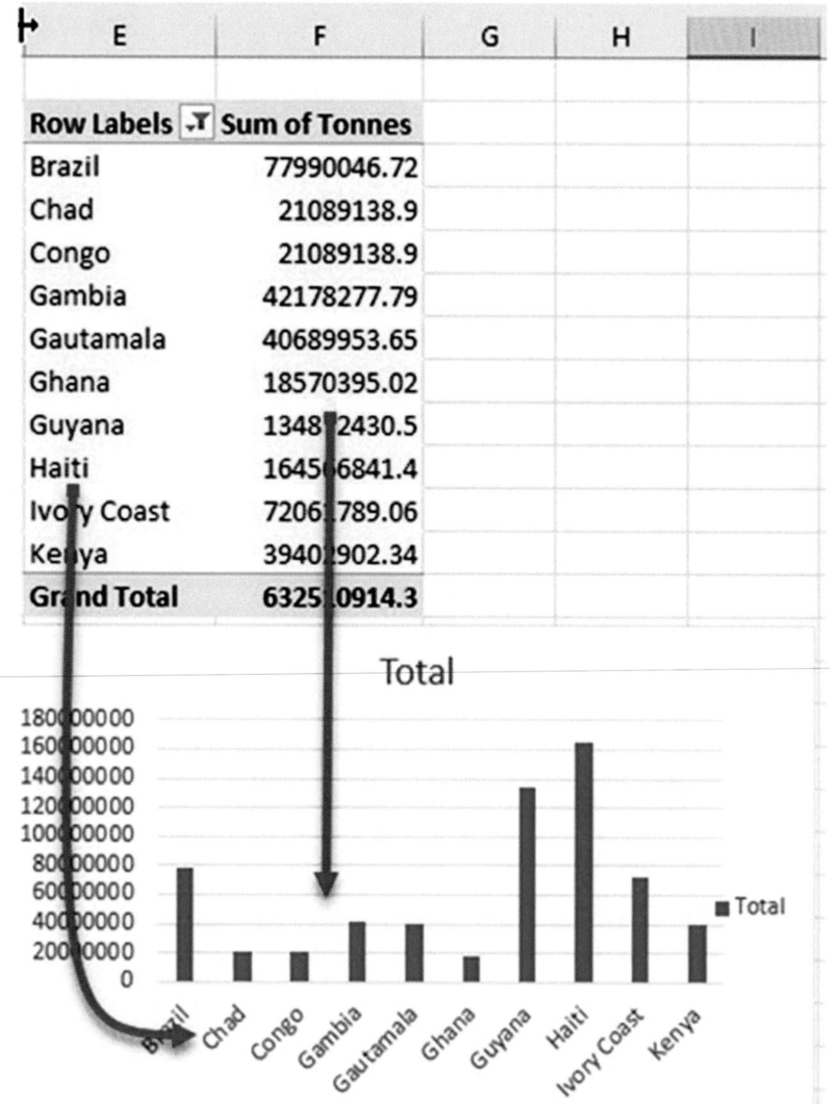

Exercise 6a:

You have been asked to provide Regional Managers with an interactive reporting tool that will allow them to easily see revenue across crops for a variety of time periods. Your solution needs to give managers the flexibility to filter out a **Producer or Region** if needed, as well as give managers the ability to dynamically filter the chart for specific periods.

Your solution is to be based on a pivot table

- Using the **PivotCharts.xlsx** workbook, start by building the pivot table in Figure 6.5.

Figure 6.5

	A	B
1	Producer	(All) ▼
2	Region	(All) ▼
3		
4	**Row Labels** ▼	**Sum of Revenue**
5	Cashew	$139,589,791
6	Cocoa	$99,222,408
7	Groundnuts	$200,312,288
8	Millet	$162,184,631
9	Shea Butter	$177,562,883
10	Soghum	$251,166,342
11	**Grand Total**	**$1,030,038,343**

Next, place your cursor anywhere inside the pivot table and click **Insert**. On the insert tab, you can see the **Charts** group displaying the various types of charts you can create. Choose the **Column** chart icon and select the first 2-D column chart. You immediately see the chart in Figure 6.6.

Figure 6-6

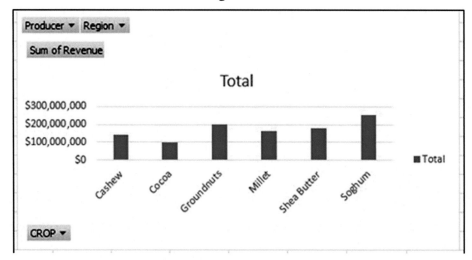

Next, click the newly created chart and select the **Insert Timeline** from the **Analyze** tab under the **PivotChart Tool** (see Figure 6.7)

Figure 6-7

This activates the **Insert Timeline** dialog shown in Figure 6.8. Here you see a list of available date fields in your data. Select the **Date** field

Figure 6-8

At this point, you have a slicer that aggregates and filters the pivot chart by time-specific periods (see Figure 6.9)

Figure 6-9

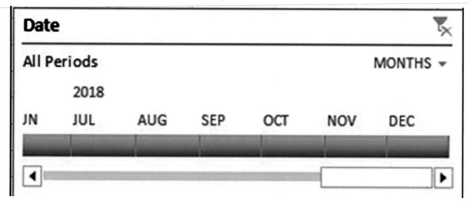

As a final step, remove any superfluous pivot field buttons from the chart. In this case the only buttons you need are the **Region** and **Producer** dropdowns which give users an interactive way to filter the pivot chart. You can remove superfluous pivot field button by right-clicking the button on the chart and selecting "**Hide XXX Field button on Chart**". Where XXX stands for '**Value**', '**Axis**' etc. (see Figure 6.10).

Figure 6-10

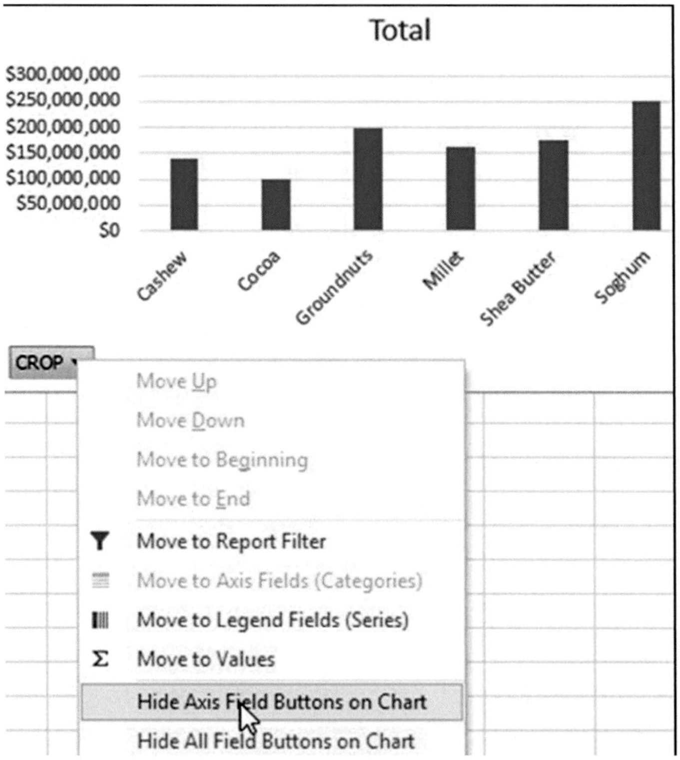

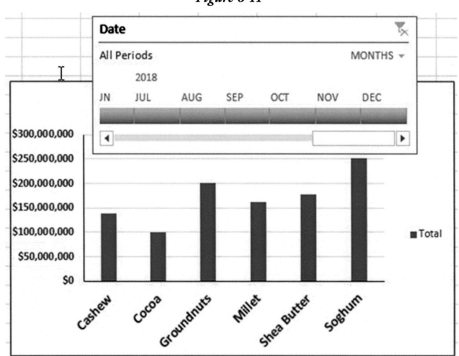

Your final pivot chart should look like the one in Figure 6.11

Figure 6-11

6.2.3 PIVOT CHARTS CAN EVOLVE

Sometimes you may want to create a chart from a pivot table and then delete the pivot table to recovery memory

6.2.3.1 METHOD 1: TURN PIVOT TABLE INTO HARD VALUES

After you have created and structured your pivot table appropriately, select the entire pivot table and copy it. Then select **Paste Values** from the **Insert** tab. This action essentially deletes the pivot table, leaving you with the last values that were displayed in the pivot table. You can subsequently use these values to create a standard chart.

6.2.3.2 METHOD 2: DELETE THE UNDERLYING PIVOT TABLE

If you have already created a pivot chart, you can turn it into a standard chart by simply deleting the underlying pivot table. To do this, select the entire pivot table and press the **Delete** key. With this method, the data behind the chart is forever gone when you delete the pivot table.

6.2.3.3 METHOD 3: DISTRIBUTE THE PICTURE OF THE PIVOT CHART

To use this method, simply copy the pivot chart by right-clicking the chart itself (outside the plot area) and select **Copy**. Then open a new workbook. Right-click anywhere in the new workbook, select **Paste Special**, and then select the picture format you prefer. A picture of the pivot chart is placed in the new workbook

6.2.4 CONDITIONAL FORMATTING CAN APPLY TO PIVOT TABLES TOO

To start the first example, create the pivot table shown in Figure 6.12. Place the Sales_Amount field in the Values zone twice. You will receive **Sum of Revenue1 and Sum of Revenue2 in the** Values zone

Figure 6-12

	A	B	C
1			
2			
3	Row Labels ▾	Sum of Revenue	Sum of Revenue2
4	Cashew	$139,589,791	139589791.2
5	Cocoa	$99,222,408	99222407.55
6	Groundnuts	$200,312,288	200312288.2
7	Millet	$162,184,631	162184631.4
8	Shea Butter	$177,562,883	177562883.1
9	Soghum	$251,166,342	251166341.8
10	Grand Total	$1,030,038,343	1030038343

Suppose you want to create a report that enables you to see the revenue from each crop graphically by using conditional formatting:

- Select all the **Sum of Revenue2** values in the pivot table

- Click **Home → Styles → Conditional Formatting Data Bars**

Select the first gradient fill icon as shown in Figure 6.13

Figure 6-13

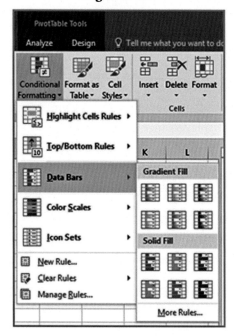

You see data bars in your pivot table along with the values in the **Sum of Revenue2** field. You want to show only the bar. To do this, follow these steps:

1. Click *Home* → **Conditional Formatting** → **Manage Rules**

2. In the **Conditional Formatting Rules Manager** dialog, select the **Data Bar** rule and select **Edit Rule**

3. Place a check in the option to **Show Bar Only** (see Figure 6.14)

Figure 6-14

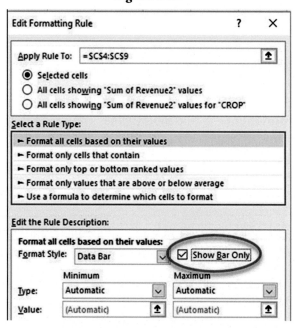

As you can see in Figure 6.15, you now have a set of bars that correspond to the values in the pivot table. You can filter the markets in the report filter area and the data bar dynamically updates to correspond with the data for the selected market.

Figure 6-15

	A	B	C
1			
2			
3	Row Labels ▾	Sum of Revenue	Sum of Revenue2
4	Cashew	$139,589,791	
5	Cocoa	$99,222,408	
6	Groundnuts	$200,312,288	
7	Millet	$162,184,631	
8	Shea Butter	$177,562,883	
9	Soghum	$251,166,342	
10	Grand Total	$1,030,038,343	1030038343

6.2.5 CREATING CUSTOM CONDITIONAL FORMATTING RULES

Use the ConditionalFormatting.xlsx for the following lesson

You can create your own conditional formatting rules. To illustrate this, create the pivot table shown in Figure 6.16

Figure 6-16

	A	B	C	D
1				
2				
3	Row Labels ▾	Acreage	Revenue	Yield Per Acre
4	Cashew	18,835,536	139,589,791	$7.41
5	Cocoa	18,517,855	99,222,408	$5.36
6	Groundnuts	19,201,365	200,312,288	$10.43
7	Millet	17,635,537	162,184,631	$9.20
8	Shea Butter	18,321,254	177,562,883	$9.69
9	Soghum	18,477,839	251,166,342	$13.59
10	Grand Total	110,989,385	1,030,038,343	$9.28

In this scenario, you want to evaluate the relationship between total revenue and dollar yield per acreage. This may help to see whether revenue only depends on the size of the planted crop or there may be other factors involved such as irrigation, fertilizer etc.

- Start by placing the cursor in the **Revenue** column.

- Select **Home → Styles → Conditional Formatting.** Select **New Rule**. This activates the dialog box shown in Figure 6.17. The objective in this dialog is to identify the cells where the conditional formatting will be applied, specify the rule type to use, and define the details of the conditional formatting. First, you must identify the cells where your conditional formatting will be applied. There are three choices:

◊ **Selected Cells** – This selection applies conditional formatting to only the selected cells

◊ **All cells showing "Revenue"** values – This selection applies conditional formatting to all values in the **Revenue** column, including all subtotals and grand totals. This selection is ideal for use in analyses in which you are using averages, percentages, or other calculations where a single conditional formatting rule makes sense for all levels of analysis

Figure 6-17

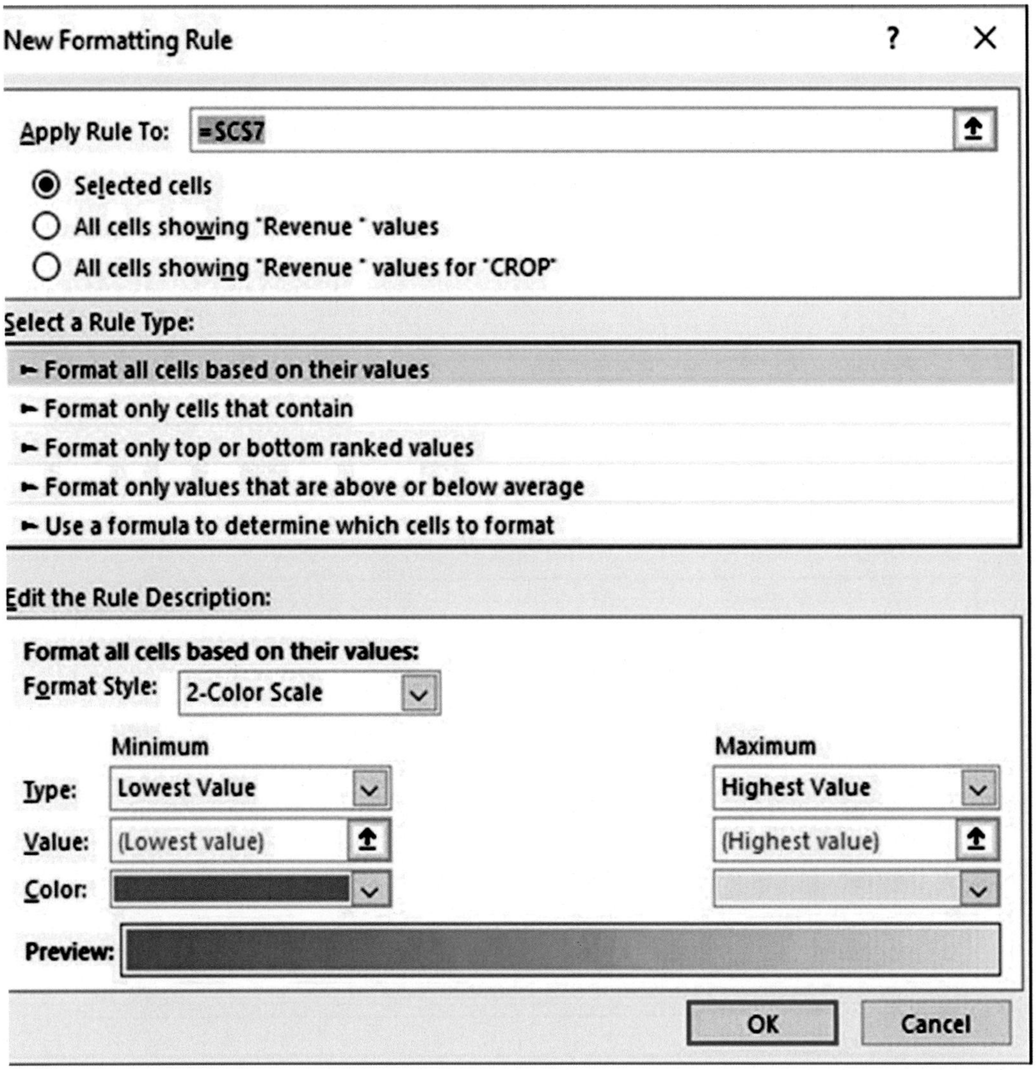

◊ **All cells showing "Revenue" values for "CROP"** – This selection applies conditional formatting to all values in the **Revenue** column at the **Crop** level only (excludes subtotals and grand totals). This selection is ideal for use in analyses where you are using calculations that make sense only in the context of the level being measured. In this example, selecting the third option (**All cells showing "Revenue" values for "CROP"**) makes the most sense, so click the radio button, as illustrated in Figure 6.17

◊ In the **Select Rule Type** section, you specify the rule type you want to use for the conditional format. You must select one of five rule types:

◊ **Format All Cells Based on Their Values** – This selection enables you to apply conditional formatting based on some comparison of the actual values of the selected range. That is, the values in the selected range are measured against each other. This selection is ideal when you want to identify general anomalies in your data set.

◊ **Format Only Cells That Contain** – The selection enables you to apply conditional formatting to those cells that meet specific criteria you defined. This selection is useful when you are comparing your values against a predefined benchmark

◊ **Format Only Top or Bottom Ranked Values** – This selection enables you to apply conditional formatting to those cells that are ranked in top or bottom *N*th number or percent of all the values in the range

◊ **Format Only Cells That Are Above or Below the Average**

◊ **Use a Formula to Determine Which Cells to Format**

In this example, make your selections as per Figures 6.18. The result is shown in Figure 6.19

Figure 6-18

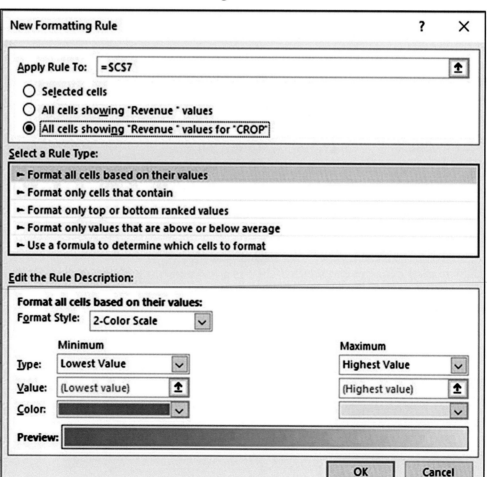

Now apply the same conditional formatting to the **Yield Per Acreage** field.

Figure 6-19

	A	B	C	D
1				
2				
3	Row Labels ▾	Acreage	Revenue	Yield Per Acre
4	Cashew	18,835,536 ⚫	139,589,791	$7.41
5	Cocoa	18,517,855 ⚫	99,222,408	$5.36
6	Groundnuts	19,201,365 ⚪	200,312,288	$10.43
7	Millet	17,635,537 ⚪	162,184,631	$9.20
8	Shea Butter	18,321,254 ⚪	177,562,883	$9.69
9	Soghum	18,477,839 ⚫	251,166,342	$13.59
10	Grand Total	110,989,385	1,030,038,343	$9.28

The pivot table now looks like table 6.20

Figure 6-20

	A	B	C	D
1				
2				
3	Row Labels ▾	Acreage	Revenue	Yield Per Acre
4	Cashew	18,835,536 ⚫	139,589,791 ❌	$7.41
5	Cocoa	18,517,855 ⚫	99,222,408 ❌	$5.36
6	Groundnuts	19,201,365 ⚪	200,312,288 ⓘ	$10.43
7	Millet	17,635,537 ⚪	162,184,631 ⓘ	$9.20
8	Shea Butter	18,321,254 ⚪	177,562,883 ⓘ	$9.69
9	Soghum	18,477,839 ⚫	251,166,342 ✅	$13.59
10	Grand Total	110,989,385	1,030,038,343 ⓘ	$9.28

With this view, a manager can analyse the relationship between total revenue and dollar per acre. For example, Cashew market manager can see that she has a low percentile for revenue per acreage. With this information, she would begin to review her farming strategy.

7. USING DIFFERENT DATA SOURCES WITH PIVOT TABLES

In this part of the book, we discover various techniques for working with external data sources and data sets located in multiple ranges within a workbook

7.1 USING MULTIPLE CONSOLIDATION RANGES

Note: Use the Export Crops worksheet in the Disparate Data Sources.xlsx workbook to follow the following discussion

Let's say you have four ranges that you need to bring together to analyse as a group (see Figure 7.1)

Figure 7-1

	A	B	C	D	E	F	G	H
1					WEST AFRICA			
2	CROP	Producer	Region	Month	Revenue	Acreage	Rep	Date
3	Cocoa	Ghana	West Africa	January	3928020.275	408796.0873	Nath	27/10/2017
4	Cashew	Ghana	West Africa	February	9250230.791	954011.98	Mike	28/10/2017
5	Shea Butter	Ghana	West Africa	Mar	1439789.97	286654.1221	Sam	29/10/2017
6	Millet	Ghana	West Africa	March	1424882.723	864359.4263	Paul	1/11/2017
7								
8					EAST AFRICA			
9	CROP	Producer	Region	Month	Revenue	Acreage	Rep	Date
10	Cocoa	Kenya	East Africa	January	3600332.184	387090.6866	Mike	23/1/2018
11	Cashew	Kenya	East Africa	February	8442285.228	779528.0434	Sam	24/1/2018
12	Shea Butter	Kenya	East Africa	Mar	2127549.251	648242.8309	Paul	25/1/2018
13	Millet	Kenya	East Africa	March	6459700.614	93866.35065	Danielle	26/1/2018
14								
15					CENTRAL AFRICA			
16	CROP	Producer	Region	Month	Revenue	Acreage	Rep	Date
17	Cocoa	Chad	Central Africa	January	1488324.143	945395.2289	Mike	29/1/2018
18	Cashew	Chad	Central Africa	February	732763.3692	4057.437398	Sam	30/1/2018
19	Shea Butter	Chad	Central Africa	Mar	4077200.277	183162.9815	Paul	31/1/2018
20	Millet	Chad	Central Africa	March	1298322.1	497955.0222	Danielle	1/2/2018
21								
22					SOUTH AMERICA			
23	CROP	Producer	Region	Month	Revenue	Acreage	Rep	Date
24	Cocoa	Brazil	South America	January	3928020.275	204389.1348	Nath	27/10/2017
25	Cashew	Brazil	South America	February	9250230.791	612364.0381	Mike	28/10/2017
26	Shea Butter	Brazil	South America	Mar	1439789.97	593087.7687	Sam	29/10/2017
27	Millet	Brazil	South America	March	1424882.723	33973.19327	Paul	1/11/2017

You can create a pivot table using multiple consolidation ranges. With this pivot table option, you can consolidate all the data from your selected range into a single pivot table.

Start by activating the classic **PivotTable and PivotChart Wizard**:

- Press **Alt+D+P (first press Alt+D together, then release your fingers and then press P)**. This activates the **PivotTable and PivotChart Wizard**

- Select the option for **Multiple Consolidation Ranges**, as shown in Figure 7.2

Figure 7-2

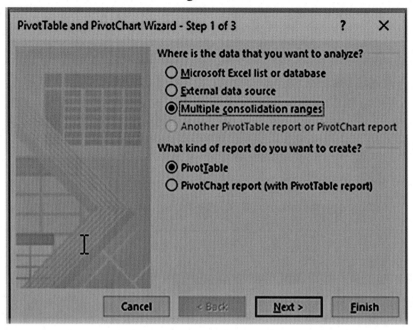

- Press **Next**, and then specify whether you want Excel to create one page field, or whether you would like to create your own.

- Select the option to create your own page fields, as illustrated in Figure 7.3. Then select **Next**

Figure -7-3

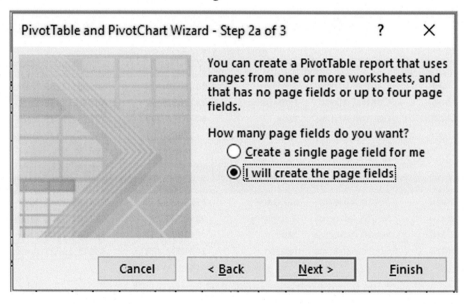

- You need to point Excel to each of your individual data sets, one by one. Simply select the entire range of your first data set (including the column labels) and select **Add**, as shown in Figure 7.4

- Select the rest of your ranges and add them to your list of ranges. At this point, your dialog should look like the one in Figure 7.5

Figure 7-4 & 7.5

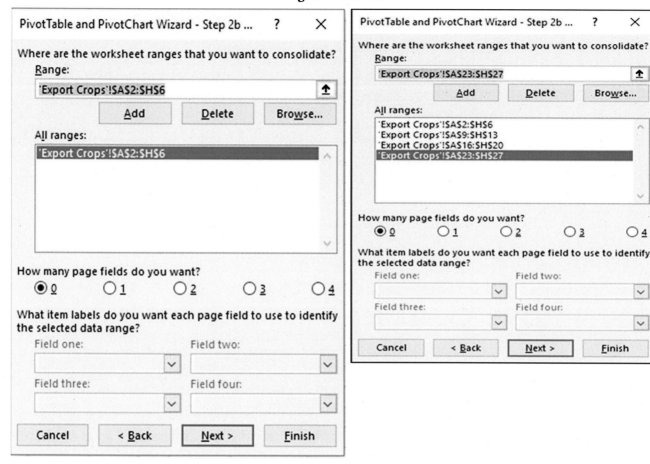

Notice that each data set belongs to a region (**West Africa, East Africa, Central Africa, South America**). When your pivot table brings the four data sets together, you need a way to parse out each region again.

To ensure you have that capability, you need to tag each range in your list of ranges with a name identifying which data set that range came from. The result is the creation of a page field that allows you to filter each region as needed. The first thing you must do to create your **Region** page field is to specify how many page fields you want to create. In this case, you want to create one-page field for the Region identifier.

• Select "1" for the "**How many page fields do you want?**", as demonstrated in Figure 7.6. This action enables the **Field One** input box. You must tag each range, one by one.

Figure 7-6

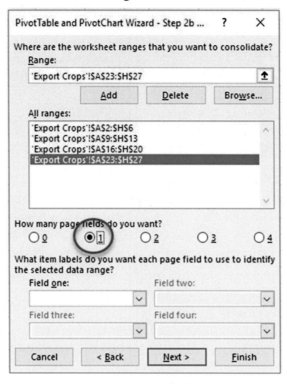

1. Select the first range in the "**All ranges**" list to highlight it.

2. Enter the region name (**West Africa**) into the **Field One** input box, as shown in Figure 7.7

Figure 7-7

3. Repeat steps 1 and 2 above for the other regions as illustrated in Figure 7.8, each time entering the appropriate field name (**East Africa**, **Central Africa**, **South America**). Click **Next**

Figure -7-8

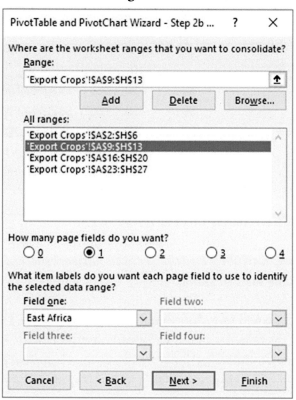

1. Select the **New Worksheet** option, then click **Finish**. You have successfully brought three data sources together into one pivot table. The result is shown in Figure 7.9

Figure 7-9

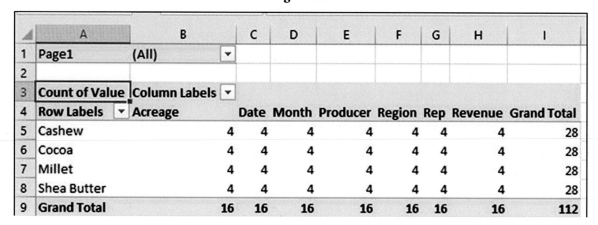

	A	B	C	D	E	F	G	H	I
1	Page1	(All)							
2									
3	Count of Value	Column Labels							
4	Row Labels	Acreage	Date	Month	Producer	Region	Rep	Revenue	Grand Total
5	Cashew		4	4	4	4	4	4	4	28
6	Cocoa		4	4	4	4	4	4	4	28
7	Millet		4	4	4	4	4	4	4	28
8	Shea Butter		4	4	4	4	4	4	4	28
9	Grand Total		16	16	16	16	16	16	16	112

Notice that in Figure 7-9, the pivot table is showing count of values. This default behaviour is due to the presence of the text data: **Producer, Region, Crop**, etc. Use **Fields Settings** to change the aggregation from **Count** to **Sum**. See Figure 7-10. Also, the **Page1** filter name can be change to an appropriate name such as **Region** or **Location** (for West Africa, East Africa…). To change the filter name, select the Page1 cell, and in the Analyse tab (in **PivotTables Tools**), use the textbox under **Active Field** (in the **PivotTables** group) to make the change

Figure 7-10

	A	B	C	D	E	F
1	Page1	(All) ▾				
2						
3	Sum of Value	Column Labels ▾				
4	Row Labels ▾	Producer	Region	Rep	Revenue	Grand Total
5	Cashew		$0	$0	$0	$27,675,510	$27,675,510
6	Cocoa		$0	$0	$0	$12,944,697	$12,944,697
7	Millet		$0	$0	$0	$10,607,788	$10,607,788
8	Shea Butter		$0	$0	$0	$9,084,329	$9,084,329
9	Grand Total		$0	$0	$0	$60,312,325	$60,312,325

7.2 USING THE INTERNAL DATA MODEL

Note: Use the Employees worksheet and the Transaction worksheet in the DisparateData.xlsx workbook to follow the discussion

Excel 2013/2016 introduced a new in-memory analysis engine called the **Data Model**. Every workbook has one internal Data Model that enables you to work with and analyse disparate data sources. The Data Model provide capability to analyse different data sets together based on relationships. This capability could rival other relational database management systems such as Microsoft Access and SQL Server

7.2.1 BEGINNING DATA MODEL

Imagine you have the Transactions table shown in Figure 7.11. On another worksheet, you have an Employee table (Figure 7.12).

Figure 7-11

	A	B	C	D
1	Sales_Rep ▾	Invoice_Date ▾	Sales_Amount ▾	Contracted Hours ▾
2	4416	5/01/2007	111.79	2
3	4416	5/01/2007	111.79	2
4	160006	5/01/2007	112.13	2
5	6444	5/01/2007	112.13	2
6	160006	5/01/2007	145.02	3
7	52661	5/01/2007	196.58	4
8	6444	5/01/2007	204.20	4
9	51552	5/01/2007	225.24	3
10	55662	6/01/2007	86.31	2
11	1336	6/01/2007	86.31	2
12	60224	6/01/2007	86.31	2
13	54564	6/01/2007	86.31	2
14	56146	6/01/2007	89.26	2
15	5412	6/01/2007	90.24	1

Figure 7-12

	A ↓	B	C	D
1	Employee_Number	Last_Name	First_Name	Job_Title
2	21	Guy	Gilbert	SERVICE REPRESENTATIVE 3
3	42	Kevin	Brown	SERVICE REPRESENTATIVE 3
4	45	Roberto	Tamburello	SERVICE REPRESENTATIVE 2
5	104	Rob	Walters	SERVICE REPRESENTATIVE 2
6	113	Thierry	D'Hers	SERVICE REPRESENTATIVE 2
7	142	David	Bradley	SERVICE REPRESENTATIVE 3
8	162	JoLynn	Dobney	SERVICE REPRESENTATIVE 2
9	165	Ruth	Ellerbrock	SERVICE REPRESENTATIVE 3
10	201	Gail	Erickson	TEAMLEAD 1
11	213	Barry	Johnson	SERVICE REPRESENTATIVE 3
12	215	Jossef	Goldberg	SERVICE REPRESENTATIVE 2
13	226	Terri	Duffy	SERVICE REPRESENTATIVE 2
14	231	Sidney	Higa	TEAMLEAD 2
15	243	Taylor	Maxwell	SERVICE REPRESENTATIVE 2
16	345	Jeffrey	Ford	SERVICE REPRESENTATIVE 3
17	403	Jo	Brown	SERVICE REPRESENTATIVE 2
18	422	Doris	Hartwig	SERVICE REPRESENTATIVE 2
19	444	John	Campbell	TEAMLEAD 2

You need to create an analysis that shows sales by job title. The problem here is that related information is found in separate worksheets. Prior to the Data Model, data analysts had to resort to employing advanced Excel functions such as VLOOKUP to handle multiple datasets. To establish a relationship between these two dataset we need to use the **Excel Data Model**. Follow these steps:

- Click inside the **Transaction** data table and select **Insert → PivotTable** on the Ribbon

- In the **Create PivotTable** dialog, place the check mark next to the **Add This Data to the Data Model** option (see Figure 7.13)

- Click **OK**

Figure 7-13

- Click inside the **Employee** table and start a new pivot table

- Place a check mark in the **Add This Data to the Data Model** and click **OK**

- Now that both tables are added to the Data Model, activate the **PivotTable Fields** list and choose the **ALL** selector, as shown in Figure 7.14. This shows both tables in the field list

Figure 7-14

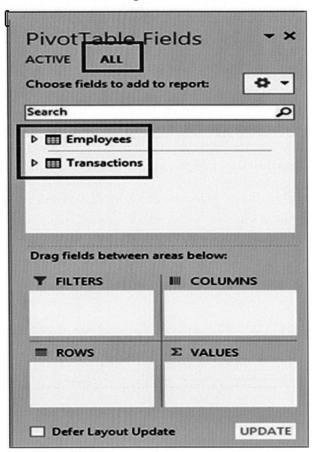

- Expand the tables to see the fields.

- Build out the pivot table as per Figure 7.15

Figure 7-15

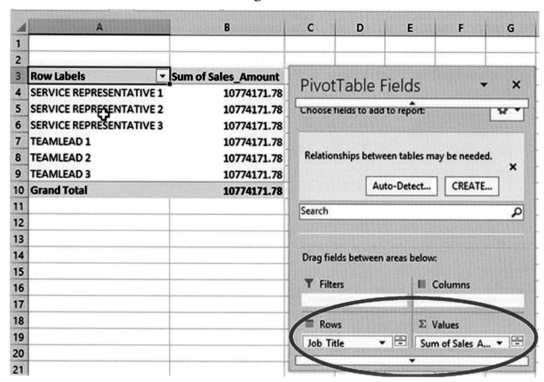

Excel recognizes that you are using two tables from your Data Model and prompts you to create a relationship between them. The fact that relationships between the tables has not been established yet produced similar sales amount for all employees. Click the **CREATE** button.

- Excel activates the **Create Relationship** dialog. Configure the relationship between the tables as shown in Figure 7.16

Figure 7-16

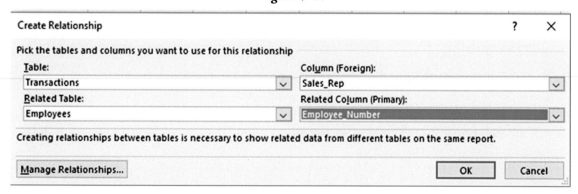

Note: You should realise that there is a one-to-many relationship between the Employees table and the Transactions table, with the Employees table being on the one side of the relationship (one employee can provide many sale transactions, but a transaction is only executed by a single employee, at least in this example). See Figure 7-16b

Figure 7-16b

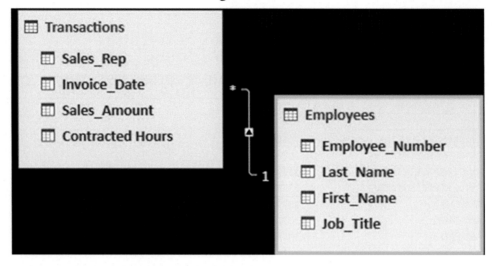

- After you create the relationship, you have a single pivot table that effectively uses data from both tables and produces the required result, as illustrated in Figure 7.17

Figure 7-17

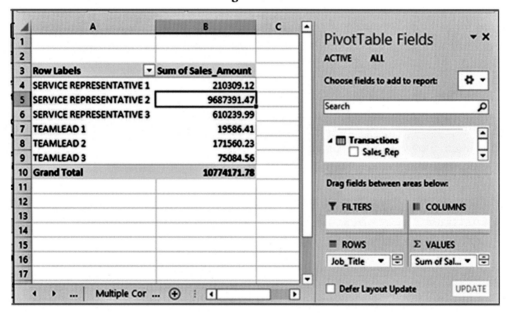

7.2.2 CREATING RELATIONSHIPS IN THE DATA MODEL

To make any necessary changes to the relationships in a data Model, activate the **Manage Relationships** dialog (Click the **Relationships** tab on the **Calculations** group). The options on the **Manage Relationships** dialog are self-explanatory. See Figure 7.18

Figure 7-18

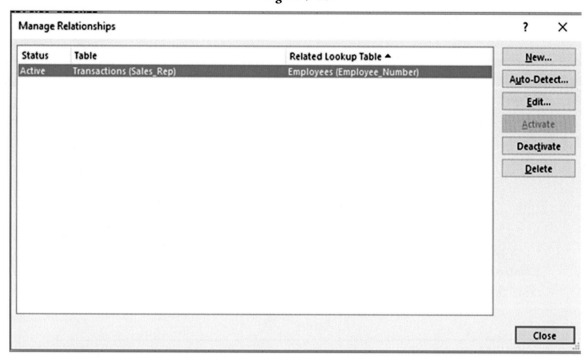

7.2.3 ADDING A NEW TABLE TO THE DATA MODEL

A new table can be added to the Data Model in one of two ways:

1. Create a pivot table from the new table. Then choose **Add This Data to the Data Model** option. After the table has been added, you can open the **Manage Relationships** dialog and create the needed relationship

2. Manually define the table and add it to the data Model

    a. Create a table from your data range (Place your cursor inside your data table and press **Ctrl+T**). The dialog box shown in Figure 7-18a appears. Here you specify the range of your data. Excel then turns the range into a defined table that the data Model can recognize.

Figure 7-18a

    b. On the **Table Tools → Design** tab, optionally change the **Table Name** field (in the **Properties** group). For this example, use *MyTable*

c. Select Data → Connection to open the Workbook Connection dialog shown in Figure 7-19

Figure 7-19

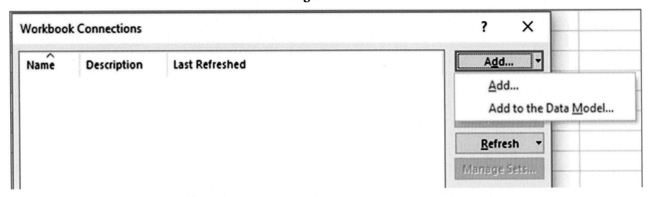

d. Click the dropdown arrow next to **Add** and choose the **Add to the Data Model** option. The **Existing Connection** dialog (Figure 7.20) opens. On the **Table** tab, select the newly created table (**MyTable**, in Figure 7.20). Click the **Open** button and add it to the **Data Model**

Figure 7-20

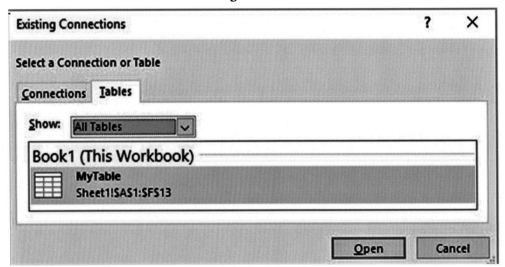

e. At this point all pivot tables built on the Data Model are updated to reflect the new table.

7.2.4 REMOVING A TABLE FROM THE DATA MODEL

To remove a table or data source from the Data Model:

1. Click **Data Connection**. The **Workbook Connection** dialog shown in Figure 7.19 above

2. Click the table you want to remove from the Data Model and then click the **Remove** button

7.2.5 CREATE NEW PIVOT TABLE FROM YOUR DATA MODEL

To create a pivot table using the existing internal Data Model as data source, follow these steps:

• Activate the **Create PivotTable** dialog by clicking **Insert → PivotTable.** Click the **Use an External Data Source** option. Then click **Choose Connection**. See Figure 7.21

Figure 7-21

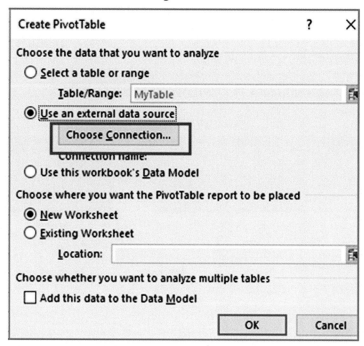

- You get **Existing Connection** dialog shown in Figure 7.22. On the Table tab, select **Tables in Workbook Data Model** and click the **Open** button

Figure 7-22

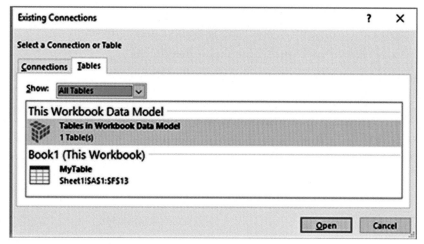

- You are taken back to the **Create PivotTable** dialog. From here, you can click the **OK** button to create the pivot table

7.3 BUILDING A PIVOT TABLE USING EXTERNAL DATA SOURCES

Note: Use the Services.accdb MS Access database for the following exercises

Excel is usually used as a presentation layer that gets its data from a data management layer such as **SQL Server** or **Access**. It is therefore necessary to find a way to pass data from the data management layer to Excel.

7.3.1 BUILDING A PIVOT TABLE WITH MICROSOFT ACCESS DATA

To use an Access data in Excel, without importing it, follow these steps:

1. Open Excel and start a new workbook

2. Click **Data → Get External Data → From Access** (see Figure 7.23)

Figure 7-23

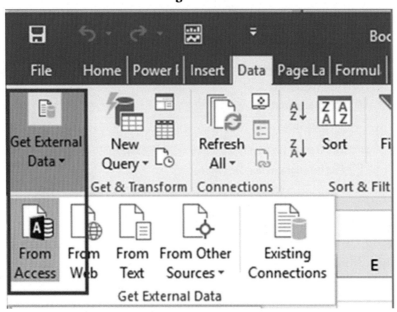

1. Navigate to the location of your Access database and open it. In this example, open the **Services. accdb**. The dialog shown in Figure 7.24 then opens. This lists all the tables and queries in the database. Select the query called **Sales** and click the **OK** button

Figure 7-24

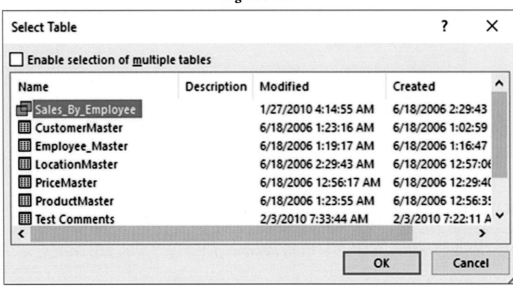

2. In the **Import Data** dialog, (see Figure 7.25), select the format in which you want to import the data. Select the **PivotTable Report** option and click **OK**

Figure 7-25

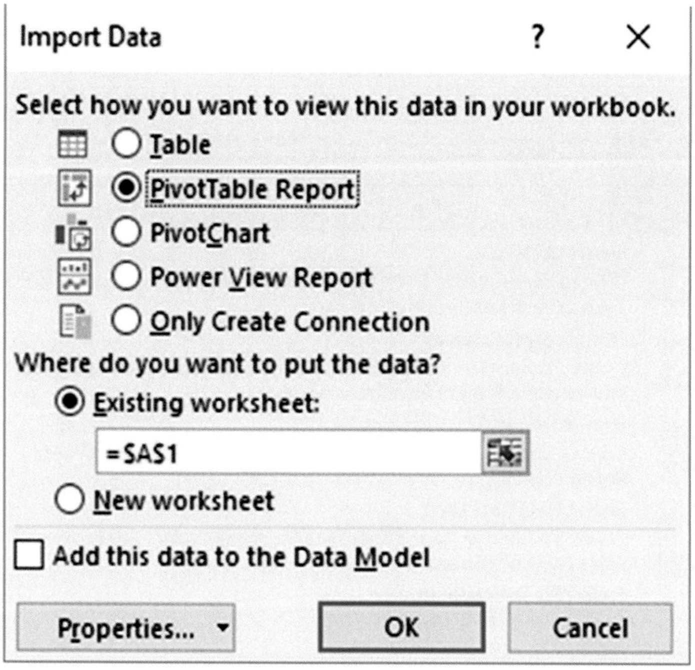

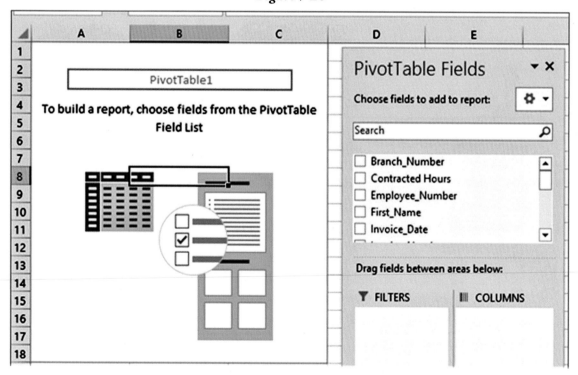

3. The PivotTable Fields list shown in Figure 7.26 appears. You can then create the pivot table as normal

Figure 7-26

7.3.2 BUILDING A PIVOT TABLE WITH SQL SERVER DATA

To follow the discussion in this section, download and install the AdventureWorks2014 SQL Server database. You must have an instance of SQL Server installed on your computer.

- Select **Data** → **Get External Data** → **From Other Sources** to get the dropdown menu shown in Figure 7.27

Figure 7-27

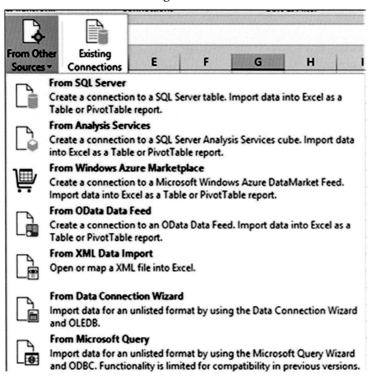

- Select **SQL Server**. This activates the **Data Connection Wizard**, as shown in Figure 7.28. The idea here is that you configure your connection settings so Excel can establish a link to the server.

Figure 7-28

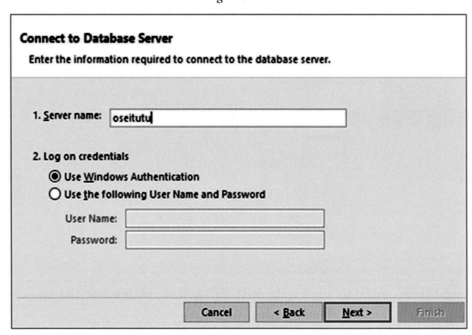

- Provide the required authentication information and click **Next**

- Select the **AdventureWorks2014** database as shown in Figure 7.29 and then select the tables to work with and click Next

Figure 7-29

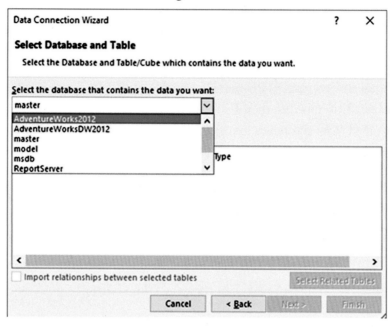

Exercise 7a:

You have an Access database that contains a normalized set of tables. You want to analyse the data in the database in Excel. You decide you want to use the new Excel Data Model to expose the data through a pivot table. Follow these steps:

◊ Click the **Data** tab and look for the group called **Get External Data**. Here, you find the From Access selection, as shown in Figure 7.30

Figure 7-30

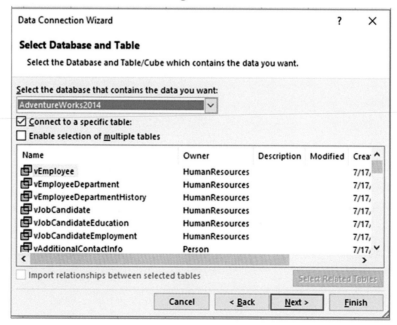

◊ Browse to your target Access database and open it. The select Data dialog open

◊ In the dialog, place a check next to **Enable Selection of Multiple Tables**

◊ Place a check next to each table you want to bring into the internal Data Model. Click the OK button.

◊ At this point, the Import Data dialog shown in Figure 7-25 opens.

◊ Click the dropdown arrow next to **Properties** and remove the check next to **Import Relationships Between Tables**. This ensures that Excel does not output a wrong relationship because of misinterpretation of how the tables are related. In other words, you want to create relationship yourself

◊ Still in the **Import Data** dialog, choose the **PivotTable Report** option and click **OK** to create the base pivot

◊ Click the **Data** tab in the Ribbon and choose the **Relationships** command, this activates the **Manage Relationships** dialog shown in Figure 7.18

◊ Create the required relationships and then click the Close button

8. INTRODUCING POWERPIVOT

PowerPivot is an Excel add-in from Excel 2010 onwards run by the PowerPivot data model engine. We have already referred to the Data Model earlier in the book. Using the Data Model in Excel only gives you limited features. Many more features require the PowerPivot add-in. This add-in ships with Office Professional Plus, or you can get it with a subscription of Office 365 Business.

8.1 JOINING MULTIPLE TABLES USING THE DATA MODEL FROM EXCEL 2013/2016

This lesson is based on Data Model.xlsx workbook

When Excel 2013/2016 refers to the Data Model, you are using the PowerPivot engine

8.1.1 PREPARING DATA FOR USE IN THE DATA MODEL

You should always use named tables before embarking on using the data Model to join multiple tables. This stops Excel from using generic names such as "Table1, Table2" etc. in the Data Model

Figure 8-1 shows two ranges of data in Excel. The first table contains crop production data set and the second (smaller) table contains country lookup table to add the product type for each country. You would like to create a pivot table showing revenue by product.

Figure 8-1

	A	B	C	D	E	F	G	H
1	Country	Quantity	Revenue	COGS	Profit		Country	Product
2	Madagascar	954	22810	10213	12597		Madagascar	Cocoa
3	Zimbabwe	124	2257	998	1259		Zimbabwe	Coffee
4	Other	425	9152	4083	5069		Other	Kola
5	Zambia	773	18552	7883	10669		Zambia	Cocoa
6	Guatamala	401	8456	3389	5067		Guatamala	Shea Butter
7	Congo	1035	21730	9839	11891		Congo	Kola
8	Guatamala	750	16416	6768	9648		Mali	Cocoa
9	Other	901	21438	9209	12229		Nigeria	Kola
10	Mali	342	6267	2541	3726		Senegal	Shea Butter
11	Nigeria	91	2401	1031	1370		Brazil	Coffee
12	Zimbabwe	547	9345	4239	5106		Ivory Coast	Shea Butter
13	Senegal	558	11628	5093	6535		Uganda	Food
14	Zimbabwe	100	2042	983	1059		Madagascar	Kola
15	Zambia	250	3552	1696	1856		Gambia	Kola

You have two options: You can bring the product data into the main Production table by using VLOOKUP (=**VLOOKUP([@Country], product,2, FALSE)**). This option works for a small data set like this, but for millions of production records and tens of columns in the lookup table the lookup solution quickly becomes impractical. The second option is to use the PowerPivot engine in the Data Model to join the table without the overhead of VLOOKUP.

Convert the two datasets to tables. Name the first table "**Production**" and the second table "**Lookup**"

8.1.2 ADDING THE FIRST TABLE TO THE DATA MODEL

• Choose one cell in the Production data and select **Insert → PivotTable**

- In the **Create PivotTable** dialog, choose the check box for **Add This Data to the Data Model**. Remember that **Data Model** is synonymous with **PowerPivot**. Click **OK**. Excel converts and loads the data into the model. The PivotTable fields task pane displays, but is slightly a different version. Note the addition of the line with choices for **Active** and **All**. See figure 8-2. Expand the Production table and choose **Revenue**.

Figure 8-2

8.1.3 ADDING THE LOOKUP TABLE AND DEFINING RELATIONSHIP

In the PivotTable Fields task pane choose **All** to see a list of all the defined tables in the workbook. At this moment, although the Field List is showing two tables, only the Production table is loaded into the model. Click the plus sign next to the **Lookup** table. Drag the **Product** field from the top of the Pivot Table Fields list to the **Rows** area in the bottom of the PivotTable Fields List.

You will notice three things:

◊   The bottom of the PivotTable Fields List is now showing fields from two different tables

◊   The PivotTable is showing product, but the numbers are identical and clearly wrong (see Figure 8-3)

Figure 8-3

	A	B
1		
2		
3	Row Labels ▾	Sum of Revenue
4	Cocoa	6707812
5	Coffee	6707812
6	Food	6707812
7	Kola	6707812
8	Shea Butter	6707812
9	Grand Total	6707812

◊ A yellow warning appears at the top of the PivotTable Fields List, indicating that relationships between tables may be needed and inviting you to create the relationship button (see Figure 8-4)

Figure 8-4

Click the **CREATE** button. Excel displays the **Create Relationships** dialog. Define the fields that are related in each table. Define the relationships as per Figure 8-5

Figure 8-5

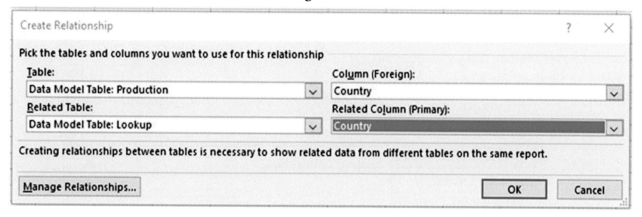

After defining the relationship, you have successfully completed the Data Model. The pivot table updates with the correct numbers, as shown in Figure 8-6.

Figure 8-6

	A	B
1		
2		
3	Row Labels	Sum of Revenue
4	Apparel	758407
5	Chemical	568851
6	Consumer	2194976
7	Electronics	222022
8	Food	750163
9	Hardware	2178683
10	Textiles	34710
11	**Grand Total**	**6707812**

In the PivotTable Fields List, choose **Active**. You now see both tables and fields from both tables in the PivotTable Fields list. You can rearrange the fields just as in regular pivot table.

8.2 CREATING A NEW PIVOT TABLE FROM AN EXISTING DATA MODEL

To create a pivot table from an existing Data Model, follow these steps:

- In the Excel window, choose **Insert → PivotTable**

- Click the **Choose Connection** button. Excel displays the **Existing Connection** dialog

- In the **Create Pivot Table** dialog, choose **Use an External Data Source**

- Choose the "**Tables**" tab

- Choose **Tables in Workbook Data Model** (see Figure 8-7)

- Expand the Production table in the PivotTable Field List

- Drag the **Country** and **Revenue** fields to the Values drop zone

- Expand the Lookup table and drag the Product field to the Rows area

Figure 8-7

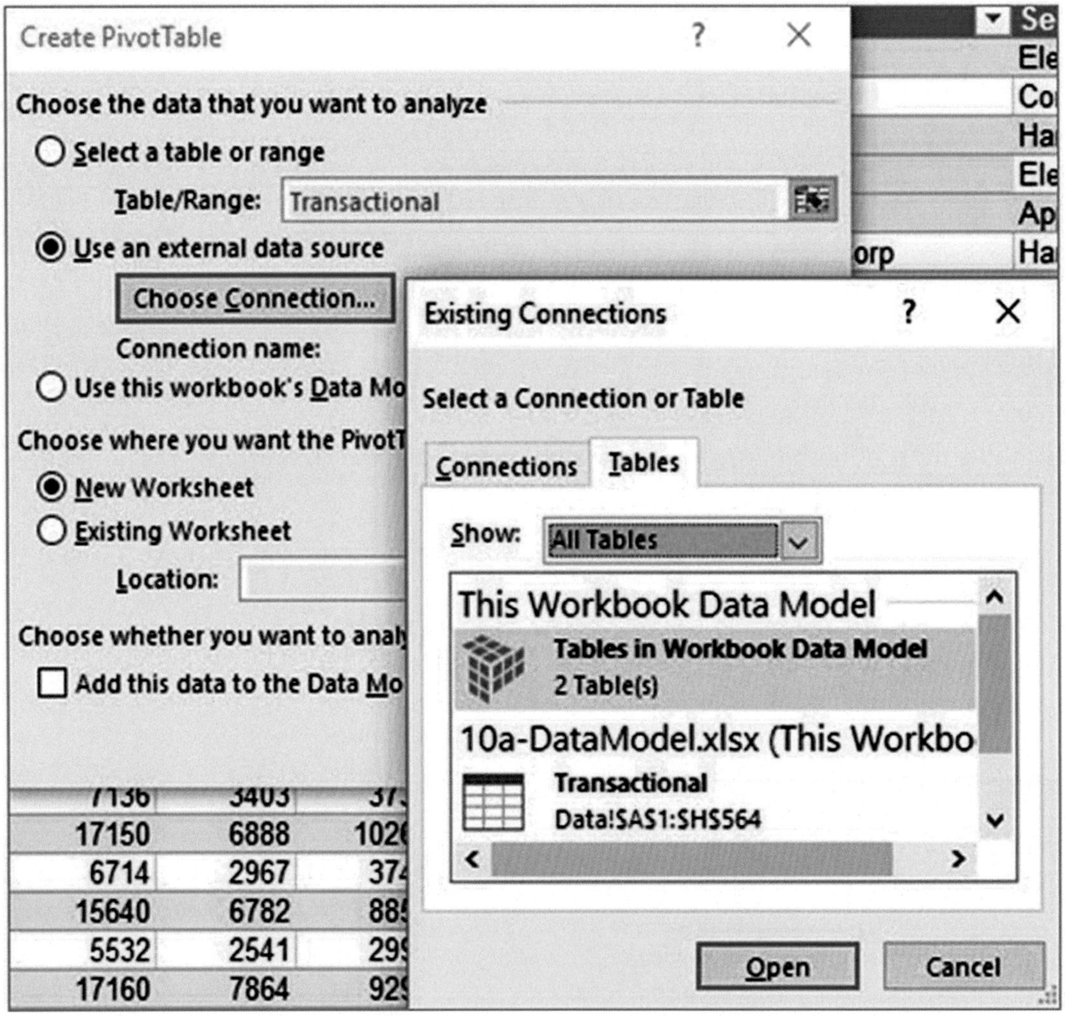

8.3 GETTING A DISTINCT COUNT

Use the DataModel.xlsx for this section

Excel pivot tables can count text values. The pivot table in Figure 8-8 is typical: **Product** (from the Lookup table) in the Row area, **Country** (from the Production table) and **Revenue** (from the Production table) in the values area. You get a report showing that there are 563 countries. This is, of course, incorrect. There are 563 records that had a non-blank country names, but there were not 563 different countries.

Figure 8-8

	Row Labels	Sum of Revenue	Count of Country
4	Cocoa	$1,632,148	144
5	Coffee	$1,009,859	92
6	Food	$704,359	66
7	Kola	$1,874,878	145
8	Shea Butter	$1,486,568	116
9	**Grand Total**	**$6,707,812**	**563**

If your pivot table is based on the Data Model, follow these steps:

- Go to the **Country** field in the bottom of the PivotTable Fields list. Open the dropdown and choose **Value Field Settings**.

- Scroll to the bottom of the list and choose **Distinct Count** and click **OK**

- The pivot table now shows that there are 24 unique customers in the database (Figure 8-9)

Figure 8-9

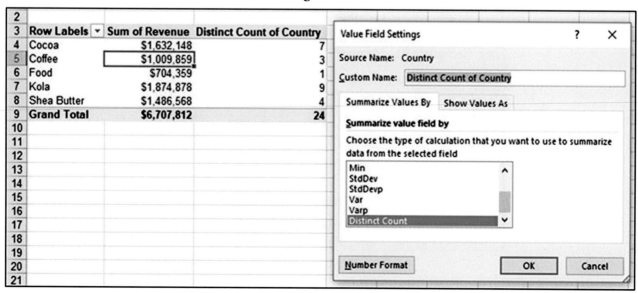

8.4 POWERPIVOT ADD-IN FROM EXCEL 2013 AND EXCEL 2016 PROFESSIONAL PLUS

If your version of Excel 2013/2016 includes the full PowerPivot add-in, you receive several benefits:

- You have more ways to get data into the PowerPivot grid

- You can import many millions of rows into a single worksheet in the PivotTable grid

- You can view, sort, and filter data in the PowerPivot grid

- You can use DAX (Data Analysis Expression) formula calculations, both in the grid, and as a new calculated field called *measure.* DAX is composed of many functions that let you add incredible power to pivot tables

- You have more ways to create relationships, including a **Diagram View** to show relationships

- You can hide or rename columns

- You can set the numeric formatting for a column before you create a pivot table

- You can define key performance indicators or hierarchies

- If you have the SharePoint Server, you can publish interactive PowerPivot reports to your SharePoint site

8.5 USING TEXT FILE DATA SOURCE

Note: Use the BigData.txt for this lesson

Your main table is a 1.8 million-record CSV file called Bigdata.txt. This file is shown in Notepad in Figure 8-10. It is important that you have column headings in row 1 of the CSV file. There should not be any blank rows/columns in the file.

Figure 8-10

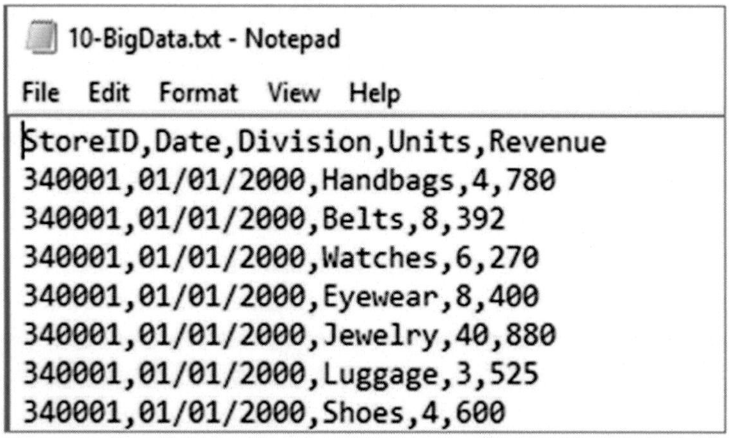

```
10-BigData.txt - Notepad
File  Edit  Format  View  Help
StoreID,Date,Division,Units,Revenue
340001,01/01/2000,Handbags,4,780
340001,01/01/2000,Belts,8,392
340001,01/01/2000,Watches,6,270
340001,01/01/2000,Eyewear,8,400
340001,01/01/2000,Jewelry,40,880
340001,01/01/2000,Luggage,3,525
340001,01/01/2000,Shoes,4,600
```

To import the data into PowerPivot, follow these steps:

1. Open a new Excel workbook and select the **PowerPivot** tab

2. Select the **Manage** icon. A new PowerPivot application window appears. This window eventually will contain a data grid where you can browse the data in the PowerPivot model

3. From the **Get External Data** group, select **From Other Sources**. PowerPivot shows the **Table Import Wizard**

4. Scroll to the bottom of the **Table Import Wizard** and select **Text File**. Click **Next**

5. Optionally, type a friendly connection name

6. Click the **Browse** button and locate the **BigData.txt** file and open it. PowerPivot detects if your data contains headers

7. Verify that the delimiter is a comma and check the "**Use first row as column header**" checkbox

8. If there are any columns that you don't need to import, clear the check box next to the headers of those columns. Figure 8-11 shows the data preview with **Units** cleared

Figure 8-11

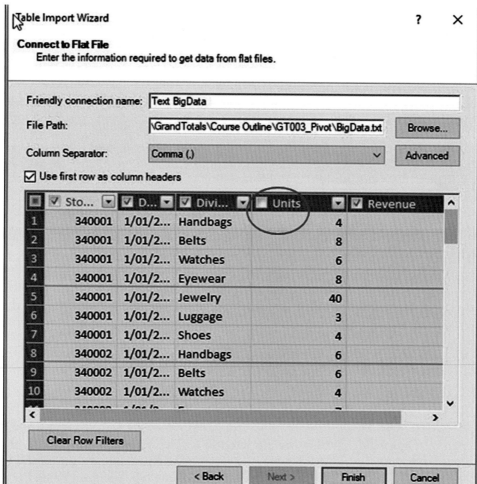

9. Note that there are filter drop-downs for each field. If you open a filter field, you can choose to exclude certain values from the import. Click the Date column filter and filter out all blank dates

10. Click **Finish**, and PowerPivot begins loading the file into memory

11. Click **Close**

12. About 700,000-row dataset is shown in the PivotTable window (see Figure 8-12). Scroll down and scroll through the records. You can sort, change the number format, or filter,

Exercise:

- Apply the currency format to the **Revenue** column

  ◊ Select a cell in the Revenue column. Click the **Formatting** group in the Home tab, click the dropdown next to **Format** and select **Currency**

- Change the format of the Date column to **dd/mm/yyyy** (without the time component)

  ◊ Repeat the above, and select the appropriate date format

- Right-click a column header and experiment with the options on the dropdown

- You can hide a column from the PivotTable Fields list in Excel or any other reporting tool

  ◊ Right-click the column header and select "**Hide from Client Tools**"

8.6 ADD EXCEL DATA BY COPYING AND PASTING

The file imported previously has only StoreID as a field. It does not have the store name or location. If you have an Excel or text file that maps the StoreID to the store name and other relevant data, you can import this data into PowerPivot. You can use Copy and Paste, as described here, or create a linked table as described in the next section. Linked tables work better.

Follow these steps to use Copy and Paste to bring data into your PowerPivot data model:

1. Open a workbook that contains the data that maps StoreID to Store name in Excel (**10c-BigData.xlsx**). To open another workbook, use the Excel icon on the task bar (at the bottom of the monitor) to switch from the Data Model to Excel. In Excel, click **File → Open** and navigate 10c_BigData.xlsx

2. Select a cell in the **Stores** worksheet (including headers) with Ctrl+A+A (press Ctrl then press **A** twice)

3. Select the whole data including the column headers and copy the data with Ctrl+C

4. Use the Excel icon on the task bar to switch to the Data Model.

   If you closed the Data Model window, click the Power Pivot tab in Excel and then click **Manage** tab to open the Data Model. Make sure this window is displayed and select a cell in the data model

5. Click the **Paste** icon on the left side of the PowerPivot **Home** tab. You see a **Paste Preview** window

6. Give the new table a better name. Try **StoreInfo** and click **OK**

   You now see the store information in a new **StoreInfo** tab. Notice that there are now two worksheet tabs in PowerPivot as shown in Figure 8-12

Figure8-12

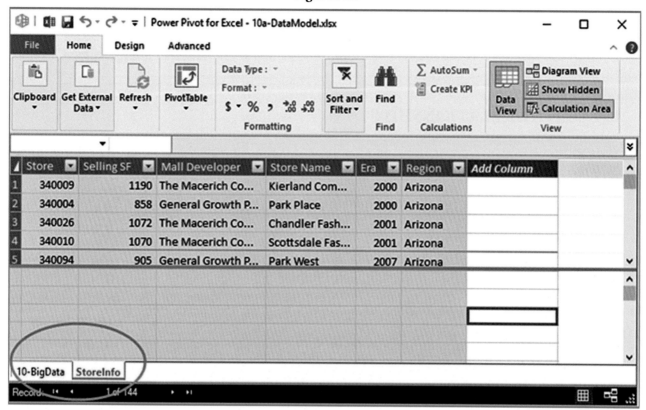

The data you have pasted is a static copy of the Excel data. If the original Excel data changes, you must copy the data and do a **Paste Replace** in PowerPivot

8.7 ADD EXCEL DATA BY LINKING

Use the same 10c-BigData.xlsx

In the previous example, we added the **StoreInfo** table by Copy and Paste. This creates two copies of the data. One is stored in Excel worksheet, and the other is stored in the PowerPivot window. If the original worksheet changes, those changes will not make it through to PowerPivot. An alternative is to link the data from Excel to PowerPivot.

To link to Excel data, the data must be converted to the Table Format introduced in Excel 2007:

1. If you start with an Excel worksheet, make sure you have single-row headings at the top, with no blank rows or blank columns

2. Select one cell in the worksheet and Press **Ctrl+T** to create a table

3. Go to the **Table Tools → Design tab** tab. On the left side of the Ribbon, rename the table as **StoreInfo1**

4. On the PowerPivot tab, in the **Tables** group, find the icon that says **Add to Data Model**. Click this icon to have a copy of the table appear in the PowerPivot grid.

Note: You may have worksheets with data that are related but are in different workbooks. If you want to bring these related datasets into the same Data Model, you need to bring the different worksheets into a single workbook. If you add worksheets stored in separate workbooks to the Data Model, each workbook will create its own Data Model

8.8 DEFINE RELATIONSHIPS

Normally, in regular Excel you would be creating **VLOOKUPS** to match the two tables. This is far easier in PowerPivot

1. In the PowerPivot window, go to the **Home** tab and choose **Diagram View**. PowerPivot shows your two tables side by side

2. Click the **StoreID** field in the main table and drag to the **Store** field in the lookup table. Excel draws arrows indicating the relationship (see Figure 8-13)

3. To return to the Data Grid, click the **Data View** icon in the **Home** tab of the PowerPivot window

Figure 8-13

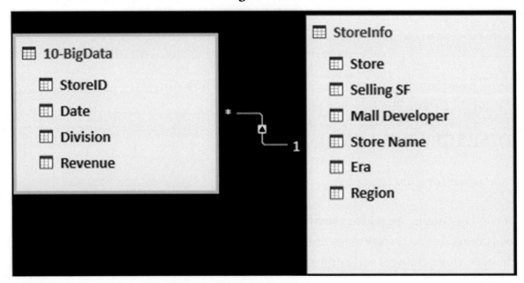

8.9 ADD CALCULATED COLUMNS USING DAX

One downside to pivot tables created from PowerPivot data is that they cannot automatically group daily data up to years. Before building the pivot table, let's use the DAX formula language to add a new calculated column to the data in PowerPivot. Follow these steps to add a **Year** field:

1. Click the **BigData** tab at the bottom of the PowerPivot Data Model.

2. The column to the right of the **Revenue** has a heading of **Add Column**. Click the first cell of this blank column

3. Enter the following formula in the formula bar

   "=Year(BigData[Date])" (without the quotes)

4. Right-click the column and select Rename Column. Type "Year" as column name

8.10 BUILD A PIVOT TABLE IN THE DATA MODEL

In the Data Model, open the PivotTable drop-down on the **Home** tab of the PivotTable ribbon. As shown in Figure 8-14, you have choices for a single pivot table, a single chart, a chart and a table, and so on

Figure 8-14

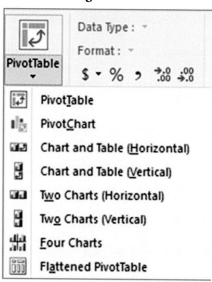

Follow these steps:

1. Select PivotTable. You now see the PowerPivot tab back in Excel window

2. Put the pivot table in a new worksheet. Click **OK**. You are now back in Excel.

3. Expand the **10-BigData** table in the PivotTable Fields List and select **Revenue**. Expand the **StoreInfo** table and select **Region**. Excel builds a pivot table showing sales by region

Figure 8-15

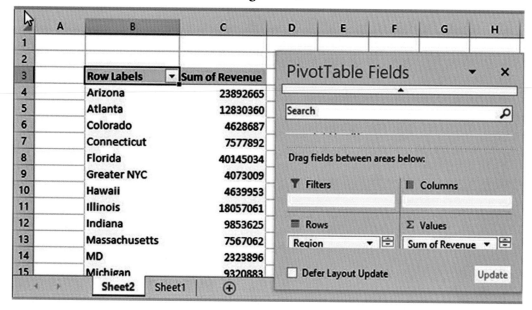

8.11 USING THE RELATED FUNCTION

The DAX **RELATED** function is used to reference a column on the one side of a Many-to-One relationship. In this section, we are creating a calculated column in the **BigData** table (on the Many side), but need to reference a related column in the StoreInfo table (On the One side). If we need to do the reverse, that is, reference a column in the table on Many side of the relationship, we will use a companion function called **RELATEDTABLE**

Use DAX RELATED function to calculate the Revenue per square foot

1. Activate the **BigData** table and select a cell within the column named **Add Column**

2. Type the equal sign (=) and then click a cell in the **Revenue** column to get the formula =[**Revenue**]. Type the slash for division

3. Type **RELATED (**.

4. Select the correct option from the dropdown as shown in Figure 8-16. The full formula is =[**Revenue**]/ **RELATED (StoreInfo [Selling SF])**

Figure8-16

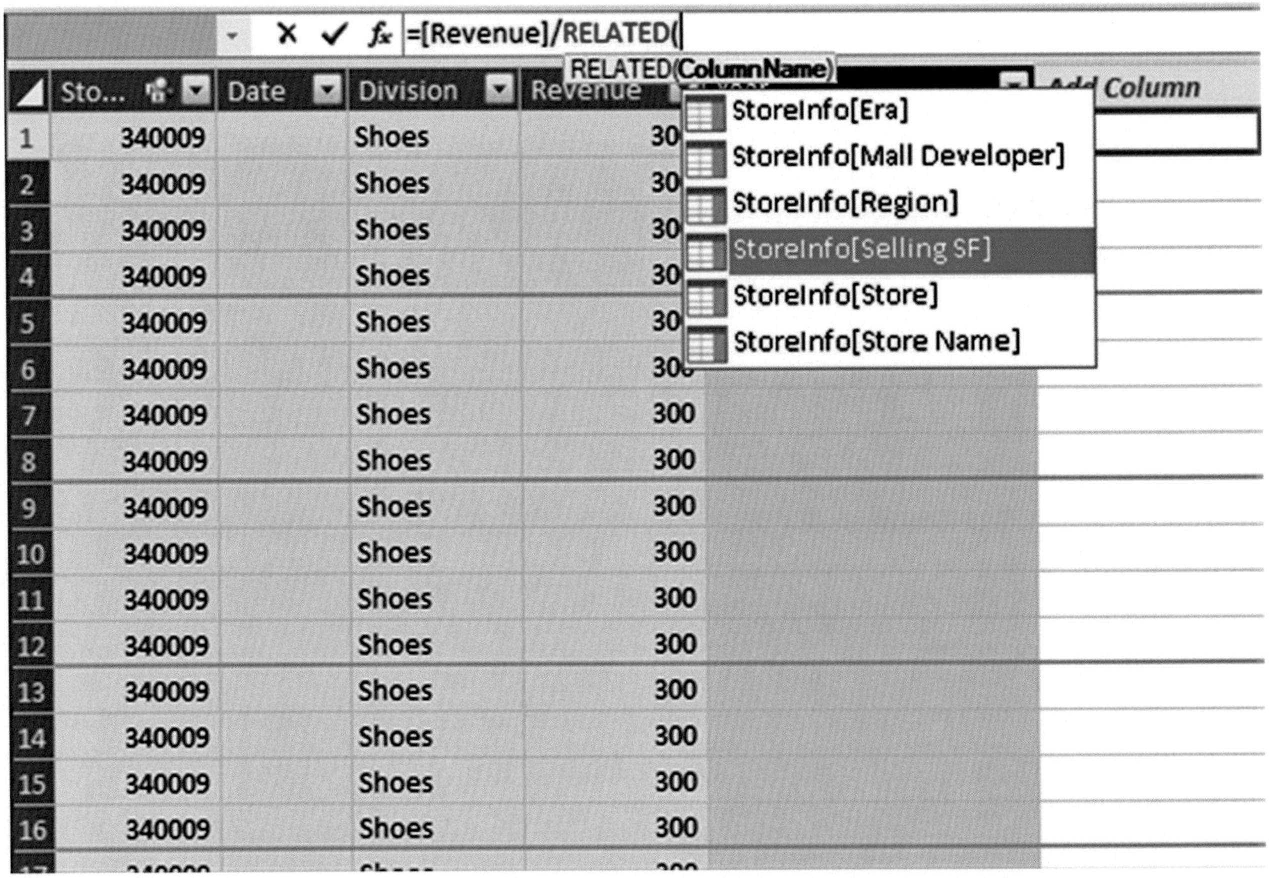

8.12 USING A CALENDAR TABLE TO ENABLE TIME INTELLIGENCE FUNCTIONS

DAX offers a series of time intelligence functions. These functions require a special table composed of dates (a DATE table). The table should have a date column. Each date that appears in the original data set should appear in exactly one row in the date table. In order words, you should remove duplicate dates. In a way, the DATE table behaves like a "lookup" table. You can add additional columns to the date table such as year, month, or weekday. You can use Excel to create a DATE (or CALENDAR) table. Here are the steps to create a calendar table in Excel:

1. Activate a cell in the BigData worksheet in Excel. Select and copy the entire Date column.

2. Paste the copied data in column A (or any empty column) of a new worksheet

3. With column A still selected, choose **Data ➔ Remove Duplicate ➔ OK**

4. Format the Date column as **dd/mm/yyyy**

5. Add additional columns as necessary. In Figure 8-17, new columns show **Year, Weekday, Weekday Name, Month**, and **Month Name**. The formulas at the top of each column in Figure 8-17 show you how to calculate the values in each column

Figure 8-17

	A	B	C	D	E	F
1		B4=YEAR(A4)	C4=WEEKDAY(A4,1)	D4=TEXT(A4,"ddd")	E4=MONTH(A4)	F4=TEXT(A4,"mmmm")
2						
3	Date	Year	Weekday	WeekdayName	Month	MonthName
4	1/06/2014	2014	1	Sun	6	June
5	2/06/2014	2014	2	Mon	6	June
6	3/06/2014	2014	3	Tue	6	June
7	4/06/2014	2014	4	Wed	6	June
8	5/06/2014	2014	5	Thu	6	June
9	6/06/2014	2014	6	Fri	6	June
10	7/06/2014	2014	7	Sat	6	June
11	8/06/2014	2014	1	Sun	6	June
12	9/06/2014	2014	2	Mon	6	June
13	10/06/2014	2014	3	Tue	6	June
14	11/06/2014	2014	4	Wed	6	June

6. Convert the data to a table using Ctrl+T

7. On the Table Tool ➔ Design tab, name your table Calendar

8.12.1 ADDING THE DATA TO POWERPIVOT AND FORMATTING IT

1. Rename the **BigData** sheet in the Data Model to **Sales**

2. Add the Calendar table to the Data Model (see section 8.6)

Next you do some formatting to the two tables:

1. Select the **Date** column in the Sales table

2. In the PowerPivot window, go to the **Home** tab. In the **Formatting** group, select *3/14/2001 from the Date formatting dropdown list

3. Format the Revenue column in the Sales table as currency (no decimals)

4. Select a cell within the Sales table again

5. On the **Design** tab of PowerPivot, choose **Create Relationship (or Manage Relationship)**

6. Create a relationship between the **Sales** and the **Calendar** tables using the **Date** fields in both tables

7. Select the **Calendar** table and click the **Design** tab (PowerPivot). Open the dropdown for **Mark as Data Table**. From the dropdown, choose **Mark as Date Table** and click **OK.** This step is important for enabling the date filters in the PivotTable Fields List

8.12.2 SPECIFYING SORTING COLUMNS

1. In PowerPivot, select the **Calendar** table

2. Select a cell in the **WeekdayName** column

3. On the PowerPivot home tab, in the **Sort and Filter** group, click the **Sort by Column** icon

4. In the **Sort By Column** dialog, indicate that **WeekdayName** should be sorted by **Weekday** (see Figure 8-18). Click **OK**

Figure8-18

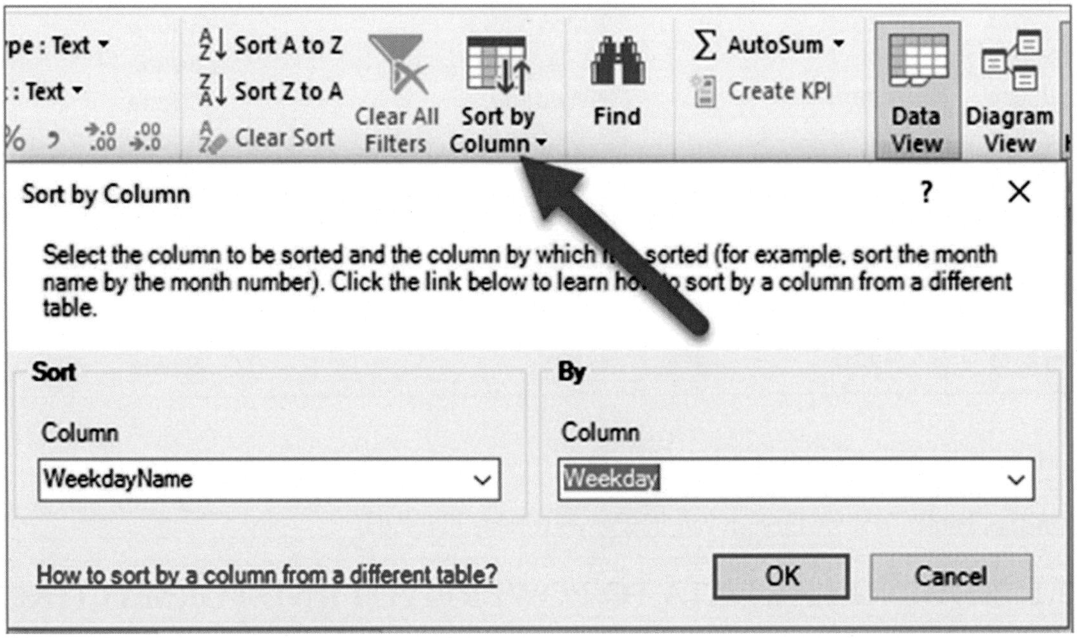

5. Select a cell in the **Month Name** column. Repeat steps 3 and 4 but specify that **MonthName** should be sorted by **Month**

8.12.3 CREATE PIVOTTABLE FROM THE DATA MODEL

In PowerPivot Data Model, select the sales table. In the **Home** tab, open the PivotTable dropdown and choose a single pivot table

In the PowerPivot Field List, expand the **Calendar** table. Hover over the **Date** field and open the dropdown that appears. In the fly-out menu, choose **Date Filters**, and you can get all the date filters that apply to a regular pivot table (see Figure 8-19)

Figure 8-19

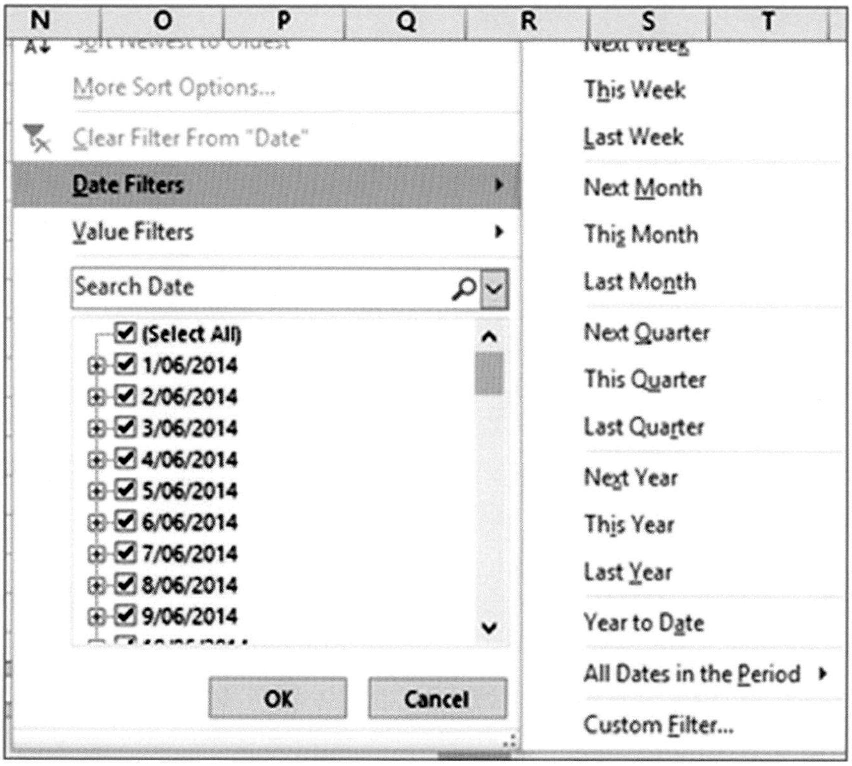

To add fields to the pivot table, do the following:

1. Drag the **WeekdayName** field from the Calendar table to the Column area

2. Place the **Revenue** field in the values area (values may be different from the figure below)

3. Insert a slicer for the Weekday and change the column to 7. To do this, select the slicer and use the **Columns** spin button in the **Buttons** group

4. Filter the pivot table for Mon-Fri

8.13 POWERPIVOT TIME INTELLIGENCE

To use the time intelligence functions, the preceding steps (steps 1 to 4 above) must be completed... Then:

1. Open the Calendar table and drag **Date** to the Rows Label area

2. Open the **Sales** table and drag **Revenue** to the values area

3. Add a slicer for Year and select 2008 from the Year slicer

You will have the pivot table shown in figure 8-20.

Figure 8-20

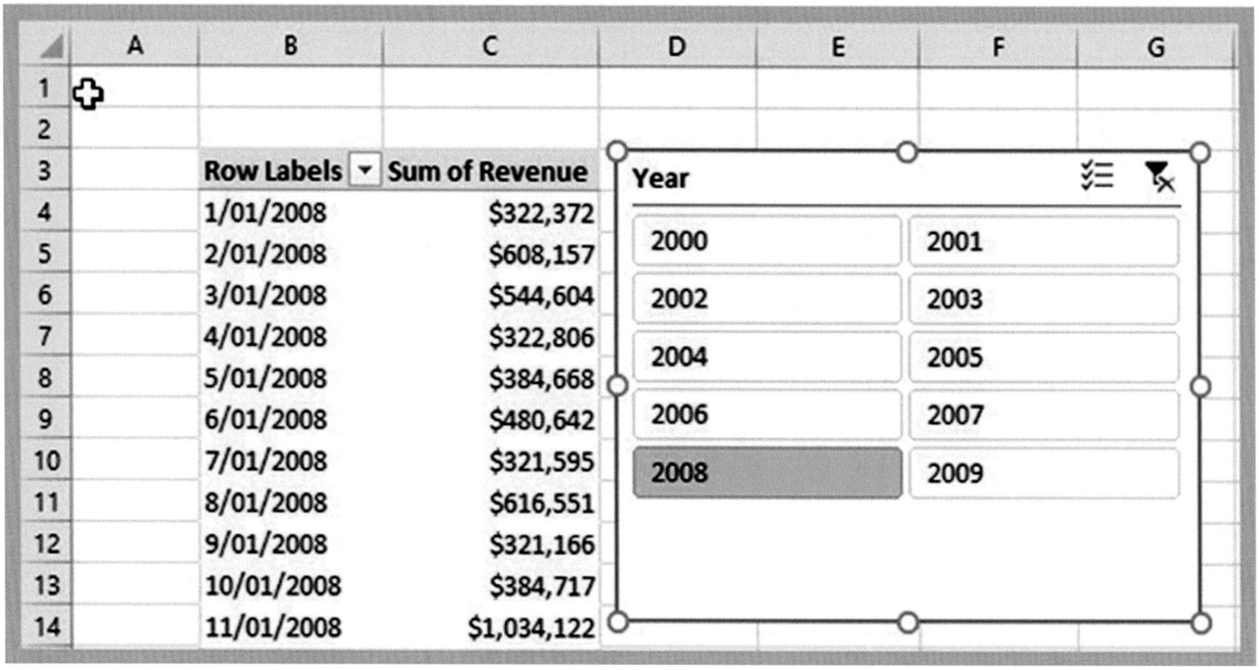

	A	B	C	D	E	F	G
1	✛						
2							
3		Row Labels ▾	Sum of Revenue	Year		☷	▼ₓ
4		1/01/2008	$322,372				
5		2/01/2008	$608,157	2000		2001	
6		3/01/2008	$544,604	2002		2003	
7		4/01/2008	$322,806	2004		2005	
8		5/01/2008	$384,668				
9		6/01/2008	$480,642	2006		2007	
10		7/01/2008	$321,595	2008		2009	
11		8/01/2008	$616,551				
12		9/01/2008	$321,166				
13		10/01/2008	$384,717				
14		11/01/2008	$1,034,122				

The goal is to build **Calculated Fields** in DAX to compare sales from this day to the identical day one year ago. This is tough to do, because cell C5, for example, is filtered to only show records for 2/01/2008. You are going to have to unfiltered the date field and reapply a filter of one year ago. And, should you require similar information for other years, then you must keep on un-filtering and filtering. The solution involves the **CALCULATE** function to overwrite the existing implicit filter. Row 5 in the pivot table is implicitly filtered to January 2, 2008. The formula to use is:

=CALCULATE ([Sum of Revenue], DATEADD(Calendar[Date], -1, year)). Follow these steps:

1. In Excel, select Power Pivot

2. In the **Calculations** group, click the **Measure** dropdown and select **New Measure**

3. Create the Calculated Field as per Figure 8-21

Figure 8-21

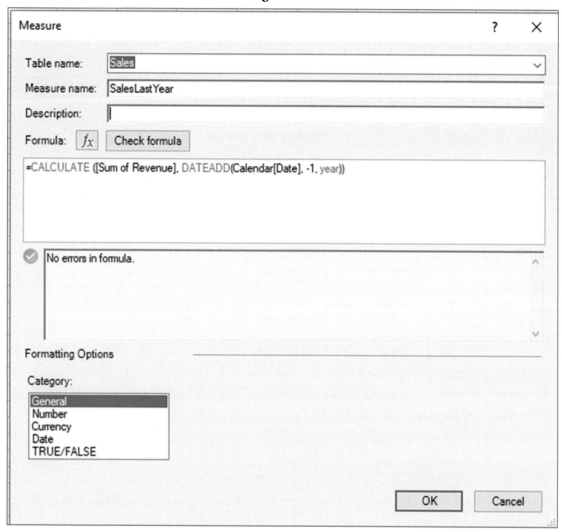

4. Format the field as Currency (no decimal)

Add a second calculated field to calculate the percentage change

1. In Excel, select the Power Pivot icon

2. In the **Calculation** group, select New Measure

3. Create a calculated field called **PctChange**

4. The formula for PctChange is: **=([Sum of sales]/[RevenueLastYear])-1**. Format as percentage (one decimal place)

9. CREATING DASHBOARDS WITH POWER VIEW

If you have the Professional Plus edition of Excel 2013 or higher, you have a new Power View add-in that creates interactive dashboard elements from your PowerPivot data. The Power View add-in allows connected interactive visualization of pivot charts, maps, and pivot tables

9.1 PREPARING YOUR DATA FOR POWER VIEW

Note: Use the PowerView.xlsx for the following discussion

The dataset for this section contains the main Fact table and Lookup tables. The Fact table reports quarterly sales data. The smaller "lookup" tables provide category information:

- The **Geography** table provides **City, State, and Region**

- The **Products** table maps the **ProdID** to **Title, List Price, Category, Version of Excel, Level,** and other category information

- You need to create a Date table that converts daily dates to year and quarters:

- Use **Data → Remove Duplicates** to get a unique list of daily dates. A new Year column comes from the **Year** () function. The new Quarter column requires a **VLOOKUP** from **MONTH** () or the **ROUNDUP** () function from **MONTH()** and a simple manipulation to convert a quarter number. After you have the date columns, convert formulas to values and add the table to the data model.

Follow these steps to create the Date table:

1. Open the **PowerView.xlsx** workbook and create a new worksheet named **Date** and copy the **Date** column from the **Fact** table and paste it into Column **A2** of the new worksheet. Sort the date into ascending order. In cell **A1,** type "**Date**"

2. Remove duplicates from the Date column (Select the Date column you just pasted and on the **Data** tab, click **Remove Duplicates**)

3. In cell B1 type "**Year**"

4. Populate Column B with the year of the dates by using the formula =Year(A2). Copy the formula down to the other rows

5. In cell C1 type "**Quarter**". This column will contain the concatenation of the year and quarter of the year such as "**2003Q1**"

6. You can fill the Quarter column in at least two ways:

   By using the **ROUNDUP** () function or by using a **VLOOKUP** from the **MONTH** ()

   We use the first option (**Roundup**) to fill the column. In cell C2 use this formula: **=YEAR(A2) & "Q" & ROUNDUP(MONTH(A2)/3,0),** and copy down the column

7. Convert the formulas to values (Copy the formula cells and paste as values to overwrite the formulas)

Add the Date table and all the other tables to the Data Model (see previous discussions) and define relationships as shown in Figure 9-1.

Figure 9-1

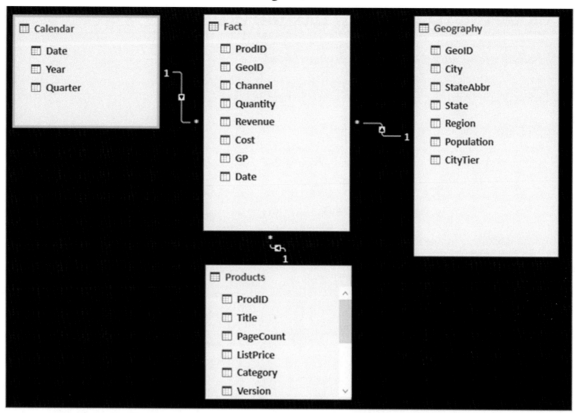

Perform the following extra steps:

Format the **Revenue** and **Cost** columns as Currency (no decimals):

1. Select the entire **Revenue** column. In PowerPivot choose the **Home** tab and then **Format as Currency.** Decrease decimal to zero. Repeat for all numeric fields that you will likely include in the dashboard. Add commas in quantity data and similar data.

2. Select the Calendar table in PowerPivot. On the **Design** tab, open the **Mark as Date Table** dropdown and then choose the **Mark as Date Table** command

3. Go to the Advanced tab in PowerPivot. There is a **Data Category** dropdown field. Mark column categories as per Table 9-1. Power Pivot may suggest these categories. If not, highlight each column (e.g. City) and use the dropdown to specify the **City** category

4. Close the PowerPivot window

Table 9.1

Table	Column	Category
Geography	City	City
Geography	StateAbbr	State or Province
Geography	State	State or Province

This categorization enables Power Map to treat the data values appropriately on maps. For example, Map will know that the City column contains city and will therefore handle it as such on maps

9.2 CREATING POWER VIEW DASHBOARD

*** Follow along with Dashboard.xlsx workbook*

Start Power View from the Ribbon. A new worksheet is inserted.

Figure 9-2 shows the Power View window

Figure 9-2

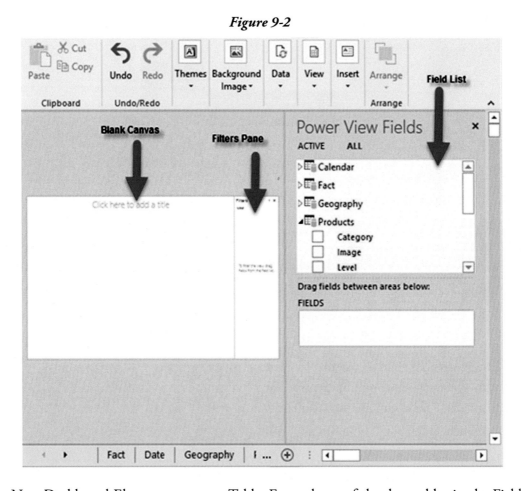

Every New Dashboard Element starts as a Table. Expand one of the data tables in the Fields list and choose any field. That field's values are displayed on the canvas. Every new element you put on the canvas starts as a table. After the table is on the canvas, you can use the **Switch Visualization** group on the **Design** tab to change to one of three kinds of tables, one of three kinds of bar charts, column chart, a line chart etc. or a map

If you have many elements on the canvas, the active element is identified by four grey corner icons. Any changes you make to the Fields list are applied to the active element. In Figure 9-3 the **Description** and **Revenue** fields are dragged onto the canvas

Figure 9-3

Description	Revenue
Cocoa & Coffee Hybrid	$20,759,220
Fertilizer-Free Banana	$159,401,010
Fertilizer-Free Cocoa	$170,325,730
Fertilizer-Free Coffee	$144,248,330
Fertilizer-Free Kola	$56,063,880
Fertilizer-Free Shea Butter	$760,638,140
Hand Sorted Banana	$3,606,525,100
Hand Sorted Cocoa Beans	$189,525,910
Hand Sorted Cocoa Kola	$1,287,139,040
Hand Sorted Coffee Beans	$179,390,030
Hand Sorted Shea Butter Beans	$300.480.240

Power View Fields

ACTIVE   ALL

☐ Σ ProdID
☐ Σ Quantity
☑ Σ Revenue
▲ Geography
☐ ⊕ City
☐ CityTier
☐ GeoID
☐ Σ Population
☐ Region
☐ ⊕ State
☐ ⊕ StateAbbr
▲ Products
☐ Category
☑ **Description**
☐ Grade
☐ Marketing

Note:

To sort a Power View table report, click the heading of the column you wish to sort by (first click sorts by smallest to largest). Second click sorts by largest to smallest

Place the mouse pointer on a table to show the Filter icon

9.3 CONVERT THE TABLE TO CHART

With the first table selected, you see a **Design** tab in the Ribbon.

1. Use the commands on the **Switch Visualization** group (Figure 9-4) to switch the visualization from table to chart. Choose a stacked bar chart. Figure 9-5 shows the resulting charts.

Figure 9-4

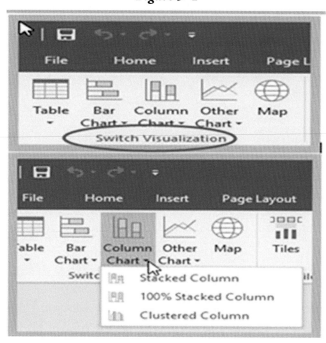

Figure 9-5

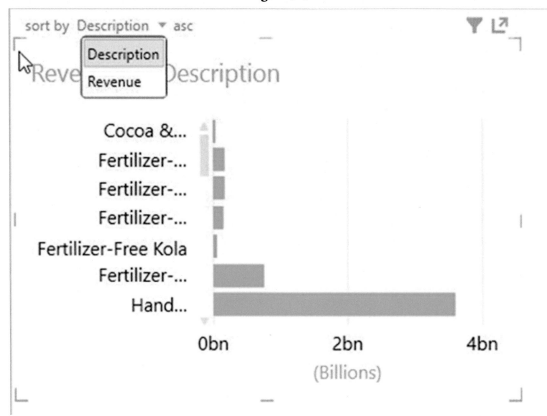

2. In the Fields list, drag the **Payment Method** fields to the **Legend** area. The chart becomes a stacked bar showing product sales by **Cash**, **Credit**, and **Direct** payment methods (see Figure 9-6)

Figure 9-6

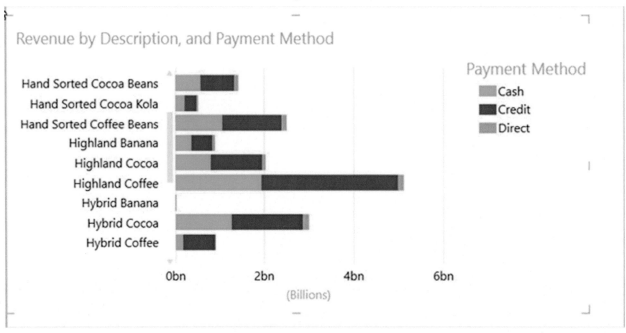

3. While the chart is selected, the **Layout** tab appears in the Ribbon. Using the Layout tab, you can move the legend to the top, add data labels, or change the type of horizontal axis.

9.4 ADD DRILL-DOWN TO A CHART

The current chart has **Description** as an axis field.

1. Drag the **Category** field and drop it as a second axis field

2. Drag the **Marketing** field and drop as another axis field

The above two actions create a hierarchy

3. Double-click the bar for the **Highland Coffee** description to get a chart of categories within the Highland Coffee (e.g. **Shelved**). Click the **Shelved** category to get all marketing methods for the Shelved category (e.g. Free Market) See Figure 9-7

Figure 9-7 Drill-down Chart

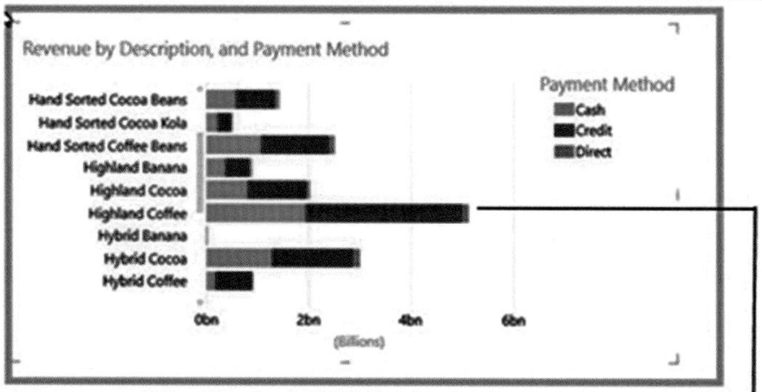

Figure 9-6a(i): Click Highland Coffee to show all Categories of Highland Coffee (e.g. Shelved)

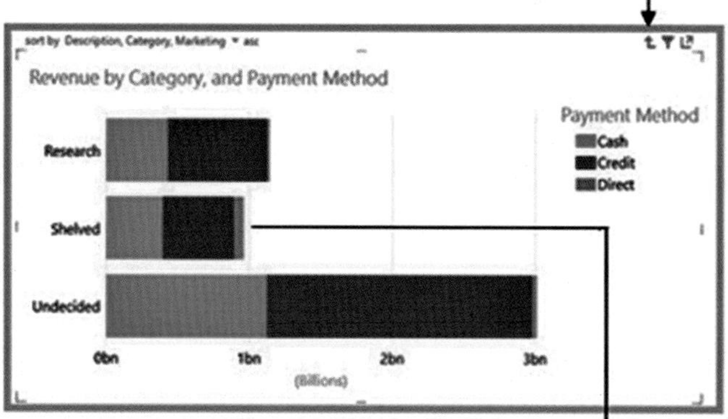

Figure 9-6a(ii): Click Shelved to show all Marketing methods of Shelved category (e.g. Free Market)

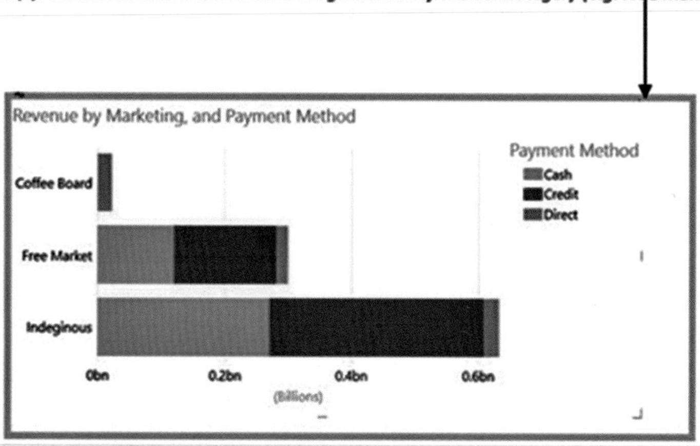

9.5 BEGINNING A NEW ELEMENT

1. To add a new element to the dashboard, you drag a field from the Fields List and drop it on a blank portion of the canvas (not on an existing element). This will display a new table, that you can change to other visualization types

2. You can also create a new element by the copy and paste method

9.6 FILTERING ELEMENTS WITH CHARTS

In Figure 9-8, two charts appear on the canvas. The left chart shows **Revenue by Description**, and the right chart shows **Revenue by Category**. If you click on any part of any chart, all the other charts will be filtered to the same element. For example, in Figure 9-8, **Highland Coffee** is selected and the right chart is filtered for only categories for Highland Coffee (**Research**, **Shelved**, and **Undecide**)

Figure 9-8

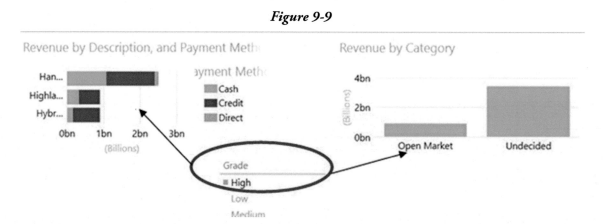

9.7 ADDING A REAL SLICER

To create a slicer in Power View:

1. Drag a field to a blank area of the canvas. The field start out as a new table.

2. Design → Slicer. The table is converted to a Power View slicer

In Figure 9-9, the two charts are filtered by the product **Grade** slicer and are filtered to **High** grade

Figure 9-9

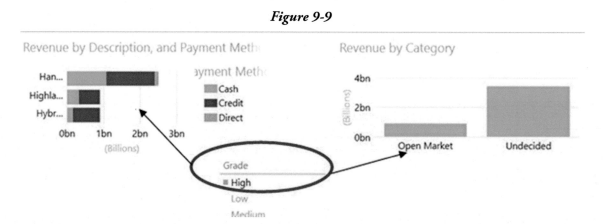

9.8 CHANGING THE CALCULATION

In Figure 9-10, the table shows the product description and then the number of market with revenue for those products.

1. Build a table with **Description, Market, and Revenue**

2. At the bottom of the Power View Fields list, open the dropdown for **Market** and choose **Count(Distinct)**

If you realize that Power View is summarizing a field that should not be summarized such as Description, you may prevent that by selecting "**Do Not Summarize**" as the calculation.

Figure 9-10

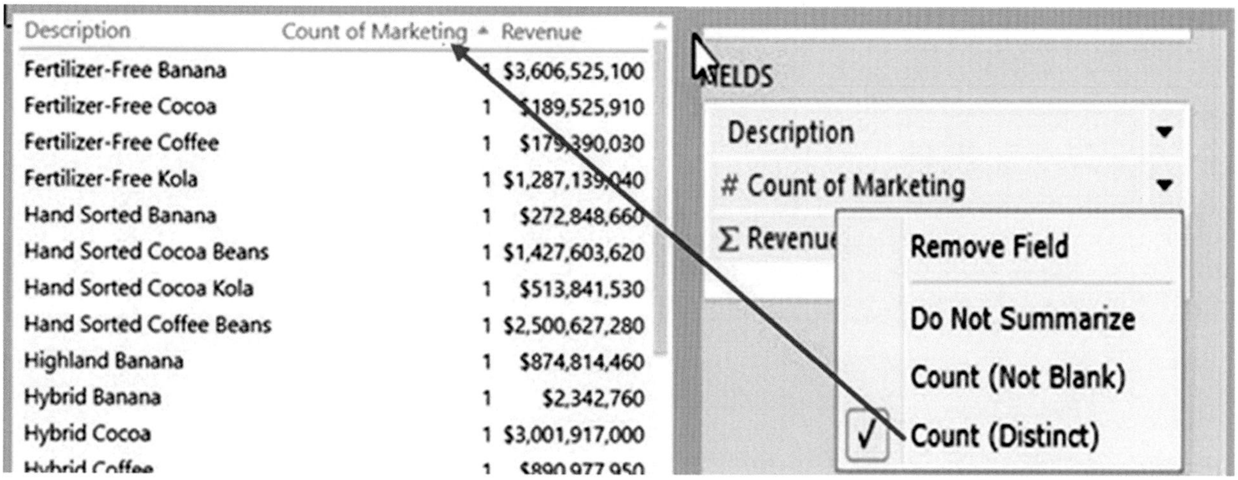

10. USING OLAP DATA FOR DATA MODEL

Preparation for This Chapter:

Before embarking on your journey with OLAP you should go through the following process:

1. Ensure that a SQL Server Analysis service instance is installed on your computer

2. Restore the file called **AdventureWorks SSAS.abf** database onto the Analysis Service instance. This file is provided to you in the exercise folder

Restoring the Database AdventureWorks SSAS.abf:

1. In **Object Explorer** in **SQL Server Management Studio (SSMS),** connect to your Analysis Service instance, right-click the Database folder and select **Restore**. Provide the information as shown in Figure 10.1. In the **Backup file** textbox, browse to select the file you are restoring.

Figure 10-1: Restoring Analysis Service Database

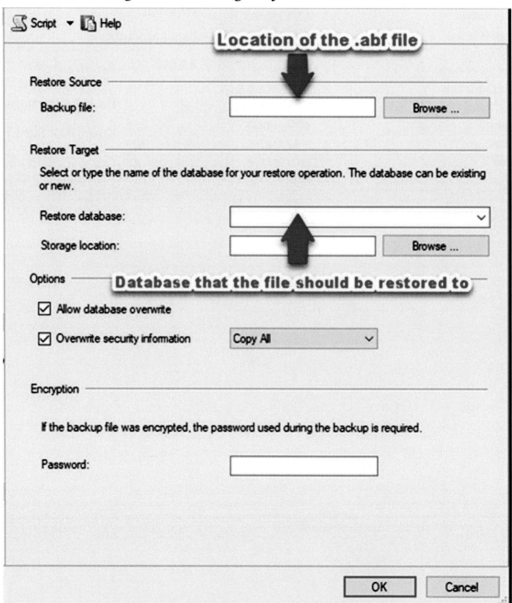

2. In the **Restore Database** dropdown, enter **AdventureWorks SSAS.** This causes the restore process to create a new database. To restore to an existing database, simply select it from the dropdown list

3. Click **OK**. Right-click the **Database** folder and select **Refresh**. The AdventureWorks SSAS database will appear

4. Close the SSMS

Online Analytical Processing, or OLAP is a category of data warehouse that enables you to mine and analyse vast amount of data with ease and efficiency. OLAP databases are designed specifically for reporting and data mining. Table 10.2 highlights the differences between an OLTP and OLAP databases

Table 10.2

Online Transaction Processing (OLTP)	Online Analytical Processing (OLAP)
Data routinely added, deleted, updated	Snapshot of data, archived, for reporting
Many tables, multiple relationships	Relationships predefined within OLAP cubes
Raw data in raw form, sorting and grouping on the fly	OLAP Cubes in views that are already organized and aggregated

10.1 CONNECTING TO AN OLAP CUBE

Before you browse an OLAP data, you must first connect to an OLAP cube.

1. Start on the Data tab and select **From Other Sources** to see the dialog shown in Figure 10.2 Select the **From Analysis Service** option

Figure 10.2

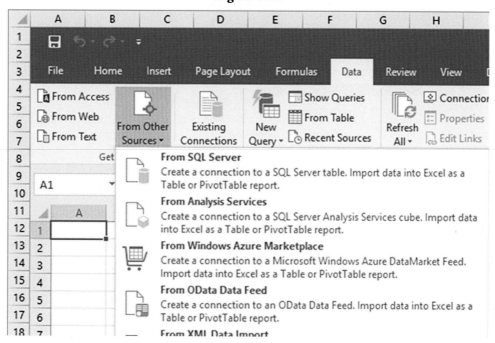

2. Provide Excel with some authentication information. See Figure 10.3

Figure 10.3

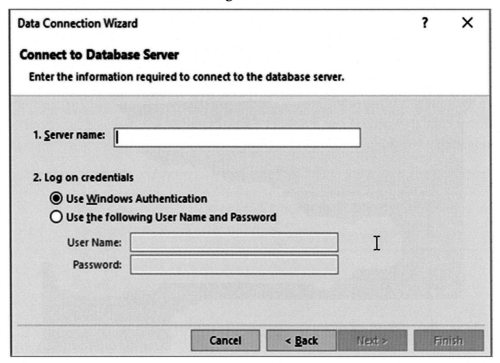

3. Select the OLAP database to work with. As Figure 10.4 shows, the AdventureWorks SSAS database is selected. Selecting this database causes all the available OLAP cubes and perspectives to be exposed in the list of objects below the dropdown menu

Figure 10.4

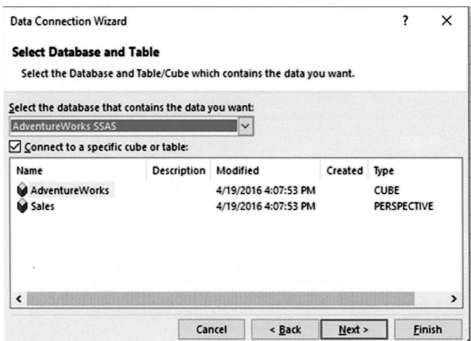

1. Choose the cube or perspective you want to analyse and then click **Next**

2. On the next screen, shown in Figure 10.5, enter the descriptive information about the connection

Figure 10.5

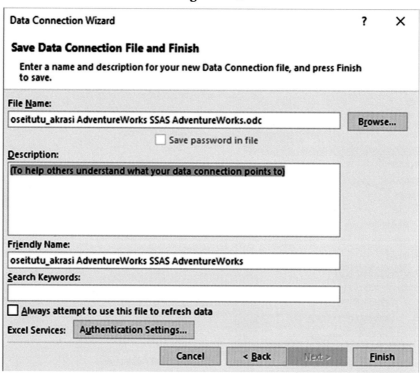

3. Click the Finish button to finalize the connection settings and receive the Import Data dialog for the pivot table. See Figure 10.6

Figure 10.6

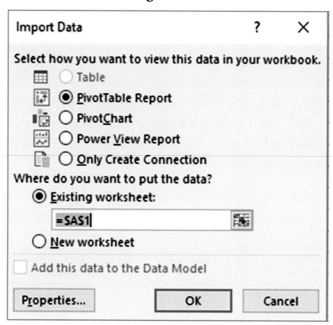

10.2 UNDERSTANDING THE STRUCTURE OF AN OLAP CUBE

When your pivot table is created, you might notice that the PivotTable Fields list looks somewhat different from that of a standard pivot table. The reason is that the PivotTable Fields list for an OLAP pivot table is arranged to represent the structure of the OLAP cube you are connected to. Figure 10.7 illustrates the basic structure of a typical OLAP cube.

Figure 10.7

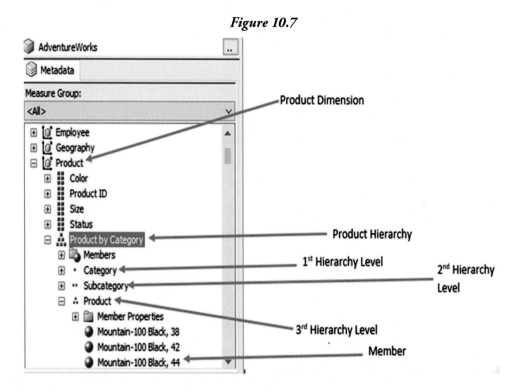

The main components of an OLAP cube are dimensions, hierarchies, levels, members, and measures:

- **Dimension:** Major classification of data that contain the data items that are analysed. In a typical Star schema, dimensions would be the tables that surround the Fact table and form a One-to-Many relationships with the Fact table dimension. Figure 10.7, shows a structure for Products dimension

- **Hierarchy:** Predefined aggregations of levels within a dimension. A hierarchy enables the pivoting and analysis of multiple levels at one time without any previous knowledge of relationships between the levels. In Figure 10.7, the Products dimension has three levels that are aggregated into one hierarchy called **Product by Category**. A Date dimension would provide a natural hierarchy such as Year, Quarter, Month, and Date

- **Levels:** These are the fields within hierarchies that provide aggregations and answers to queries. In Figure 10.7 there are three levels: Category, Subcategory, and Product Name

- **Member:** The individual data item within a dimension. Members are typically accessed via the OLAP structure of dimensions/hierarchy/Level, and member. In the example shown in Figure 10.7, Mountain-100 Black, 38 is a member (the actual product name)

- **Measures:** The data value within the OLAP cube. A group of Measures are stored in a **Measures Group** (which is a Dimension in its own right). The Measures can be sliced along the other dimensions in the cube to provide analysis

10.2.1 PERFORMING WHAT-IF ANALYSIS WITH OLAP DATA

Excel 2013 and 2016 offer the ability to perform What-If analysis with the data in OLAP pivot tables. With this new functionality, you can edit the values in the pivot table and recalculate measures and members based on your changes. You can have the ability to publish changes back to the OLAP cube. To make use of the What-If Analysis functionality, do the following:

- Create an OLAP pivot table as usual

- Select **PivotTable Analysis → Analyse → What If Analysis → Enable What-If Analysis**

- At this point you can edit the pivot table. After you make changes, you can click any of the changed values and choose **Calculate Pivot Table with Changes**. This forces Excel to re-evaluate all the calculations in the pivot table based on your edits

You may publish changes to make Excel save the changes to the OLAP Server:

- Select **PivotTable Tools → Analyse → What-If Analysis** Publish Changes. This triggers a "**write-back**" to the OLAP server, making the edited values sent to the source OLAP cube

EXCEL EXERCISES

EXERCISE 1: QUESTIONS

Ex1_Q1.

Encrypt the workbook so that it requires a password to open. Use **GrandTotals** as the password. Mark the workbook as final.

Notes:

_____

_____

_____

_____

Ex1_Q2.

Share the current workbook so that change history is saved for **90 days**. Update the changes automatically every **10 minutes**

Notes:

_____

_____

_____

_____

Ex1_Q3.

Display all the changes that have ever been made by **anyone** to this document and **not** by **when**, **who** or **where**. Don't Highlight the changes on the screen and List the changes on a new sheet

Notes:

_____

_____

_____

_____

_____

Ex1_Q4.

Configure Excel to enable background checking and display detected formula errors in Red.

Notes:

_____

_____

_____

_____

_____

Ex1_Q5.

In the **Family Budget** worksheet, add watches to the **Total row** in Difference column in each set of the **Housing**, **Transportation**, **Loans** and **Entertainment** data

Notes:

_____

_____

_____

_____

_____

Ex1_Q6.

Show all formulas in the **Family Budget** worksheet

Notes:

_____

_____

_____

_____

_____

Ex1_Q7.

In the **Employment Status** worksheet, enable the iterative calculation formula option and set the maximum iterations to be **25** and change to **0.005**

Notes:

_____

_____

_____

_____

_____

Ex1_Q8.

In the **Employee Records** worksheet, use a **COUNTIFS** statement in cell **F6** to count how many employees are in the **Perth Office**.

Notes:

_____

_____

_____

_____

_____

Ex1_Q9.

In the **Sale Orders** worksheet, use an **AVERAGEIFS** statement in **G7** to find the average unit price of **ItemSKUs** greater than **30000**. Do not include Quantities of 0.

Notes:

_____

_____

_____

_____

_____

Ex1_Q10.

In the **Sale Orders** worksheet, create a **SUMIFS** function in **F7** that will return the Quantity total of the **ItemSKU** numbers in the **10000** range.

Notes:

_____

_____

_____

_____

_____

Ex1_Q11.

In the **Employee Records** worksheet, in cell F7 add a function that counts how many people work in the **Darwin** Office.

Notes:

_____

_____

_____

_____

_____

Ex1_Q12.

Create a new worksheet named **Office Expenses**, place the sheet right after **Office Records**. In the new worksheet, in cell **A1** enter the column title **Expenses**. In cell **A2** <u>consolidate</u> the data in the **Office Records** worksheet from cells **A10:B23**, **E10:F23**, **A30:B43**, **E30:F43**, **A50:B63**, **E50:F63** and **A70:B83** using the **SUM** function. Add the labels from the left column.

Notes:

_____

_____

_____

_____

Ex1_Q13.

In the **Employment Status** worksheet, use the **Evaluate Formula** tool to find and correct the error in **S12**.

Notes:

_____

_____

_____

_____

_____

Ex1_Q14.

In the **Employee Records** worksheet, in cell F7 create a **VLOOKUP** function that finds the **ID** for Supervisor **Sam Tutu**.

Notes:

_____

_____

_____

_____

_____

Ex1_Q15.

In the **Status Chart** worksheet, change the **chart layout** to **Layout 1**, change the **chart title** to **Employment History** and change the **chart style** to **Style 9.** Save the chart as a chart template to the **the Desktop** folder in your documents folder and with the name **EmploymentChart**

Notes:

_____

_____

_____

_____

_____

Ex1_Q16.

In the **Financial Services** worksheet, add a Logarithmic Trendline based on 2005 to the **Financial Data** chart that forecasts **1.5** periods into the future. Add an Exponential Trendline to the **Other Data** chart based on 2005.

Notes:

_____

_____

_____

_____

_____

Ex1_Q17.

In the **Office Records** worksheet, modify the data validation input message for the title **Office Records** to be **Our office's income and expenses**.

Notes:

_____

_____

_____

_____

_____

Ex1_Q18.

In the **Family Budget** worksheet, create and show two scenarios named **Wants** and the other named **Wishes**, that allows you to change the **Wanting to Make** value to be **10,000** and **15,000** and show **Wants** in the cell.

Notes:

_____

_____

_____

_____

Ex1_Q19.

Create a new worksheet named **Cut Costs**. In cell A1 of the new worksheet, <u>consolidate</u> the data from the **Family Budget** worksheet using the data in cells **A6:D17**, **A21:D29**, **A33:D39** and **A43:D49**. Set the labels to be used from the **Top Row** and **Left Column**.

Notes:

_____

_____

_____

_____

Ex1_Q20.

Create a PivotTable in a <u>new worksheet</u> from the data in the **Employee Records** sheet. Display the **Office** column as the Report Filter, and **Status** as a Column Label. In the **Row Labels** field, insert the following in the same order: **ID** and **First & Last Name.** Rename the new Sheet **PivotTable**

Notes:

_____

_____

_____

_____

_____

Ex1_Q21.

Create a PivotChart on a <u>new worksheet</u> that displays the data from the **Employee Records** sheet. Do not show the **First & Last Name** field in the report. Make **Status** a Legend Field, **Office** an Axis Field, and **Sum of ID** a Value field.

Notes:

_____

_____

_____

_____

Ex1_Q22.

In the **<u>Employee Records Table</u>** worksheet, rearrange the PivotTable Fields to not show **Office** in any field and show in order: **Status**, **First & Last Name** and **ID** in the **Row Labels** field.

Notes:

_____

_____

_____

_____

_____

Ex1_Q23.

In the **<u>Employee Records Table</u>** worksheet, insert a **<u>slicer</u>** for the **Office** field. Change the **<u>Slicer Caption</u>** to read **<u>Offices Shown</u>**. Use the slicer to filter the PivotTable to only show records from Offices in **Sydney**, **Perth**, and **Melbourne**.

Notes:

_____

_____

_____

_____

_____

Ex1_Q24.

In the **Financial Services** worksheet, create a macro that formats the <u>Row Height</u> to be **<u>30</u>** points and changes the <u>font size</u> to **<u>12</u>**. Name the macro **<u>Height</u>**, and store it in this workbook. Run this macro in the cell range **A3:G9**

Notes:

_____

_____

_____

_____

Ex1_Q25.

In the **Financial Services** worksheet, create a macro that applies a <u>Currency number format</u> and a <u>Blue Gradient Data Bar</u> rule. Name the macro **Formatting**, and store it in only this workbook. Apply the macro to the data in the **Financial Data** (Note: Accept all other default settings.)

Notes:

_____

_____

_____

_____

Ex1_Q26.

In the **Family Budget** worksheet, in any open cells create a <u>Button Form Control</u> named **Set Data Bars**, and assign the button to the **Set_Data_Bars** macro and run it.

Notes:

_____

_____

_____

_____

Ex1_Q27.

In the **Sales Orders** worksheet, modify the <u>Spin Button</u> values to be between **1** and **100** and change in increments of **1**.

Notes:

_____

_____

_____

_____

Ex1_Q28.

In the **Sale Orders** worksheet, map the XML table elements with the name being **NewOrders**, to also **Overwrite** the existing data with new data and **Adjust column width**. Then <u>export</u> the current worksheet as XML data file named **NewOrdersXML** in the **Folder of your choice** folder in your Documents folder.

Notes:

_____

_____

_____

_____

_____

Ex1_Q29.

Create a custom document property named **Completed** with the Type **Yes or No** with the value set as **No**

Notes:

_____

_____

_____

_____

_____

EXERCISES 1 ANSWERS

Ex1_Q1.

1. Click the **File** tab

2. In **Info**, select **Protect Workbook**. Choose **Encrypt with Password**.

3. Type in **PureTraining** as the password and click **Ok**. Type **PureTraining** again to verify the password, and click **OK**.

4. Select the drop down for **Protect Workbook** and click **Mark as Final**

5. Click **Ok**

Ex1_Q2

1. In the **Review** tab, locate the **Changes** group, and select **Share Workbook**.

2. In the **Advanced** tab, locate **Track Changes**. Keep the history for **90** days.

3. Under **Update Changes**, choose **Automatically every:** and choose **10** minutes

4. Click **Ok**

Ex1_Q3.

1. In the **Review** tab, locate the **Changes** group and select the **Track Changes** drop down. Select **Highlight Changes...**

2. In the **Highlight Changes** dialogue box, make sure **When: Who:**, and **Where:** are unchecked. Uncheck **Highlight changes on screen**.

3. Check **List changes on a new sheet**

4. Click **OK**

Ex1_Q4.

1. In the **File** tab, click **Options**. Select the **Formulas** tab.

2. Under **Error Checking**, click to **Enable background error checking**.

3. Change the colour drop down to **Red**

4. Click **Ok**

Ex1_Q5

1. In the **Formulas** tab, **Formula Auditing** group, select **Watch Window**

2. Click **Add watch...**

3. Select cell **D18** and click **Add**

4. Repeat steps 2 and 3, using cells **D30**, **D40**, and **D50**

Ex1_Q6

1. In the **Formulas** tab, locate the **Formula Auditing** group and select **Show Formulas**

Ex1_Q7

1. In the **File** tab, select **Options**, and choose the **Formulas** tab

2. Under **Calculation Options**, check **Enable iterative calculations**

3. In **Maximum iterations**, enter **25**, and in **Maximum change** enter **.005**

4. Click **Ok**

Ex1_Q8

1. In the **Employee Record** worksheet, select cell **F6**. Select the **Formulas** tab, locate the **Function Library** group, and select **Insert Function**.

2. Search for **COUNTIFS**, and select it.

3. In **Criteria range 1:** select or type **B7:B39**. In **Criteria:** type **employee**.

4. In **Criteria range 2:** select or type **D7:D39**. In **Criteria** type **Perth**.

5. Click **Ok**.

Ex1_Q9

In the Sale Orders worksheet, use an AVERAGEIFS statement in G7 to find the average unit price of ItemSKUs greater than 30000. Do not include Quantities of 0.

1. In the Formulas tab, locate the Function Library group, and click Insert Function.

2. In the Search box, type AVERAGEIFS, select it from the results, and click OK

3. In the Average range box, enter D5:D24.

4. In the Criteria_range1 box, enter B5:B24

5. In the Criteria1 box, enter ">30000"

6. In the Criteria_range2 box, enter C5:C24

7. In the Criteria2 box, enter ">0"

8. Click OK

Ex1_Q10.

1. In the **Sale Orders** worksheet, select cell **F7**. In the **Formulas** tab, go to the **Function Library** group and click **Insert Function**.

2. In the **Insert Function** window, enter **SUMIFS** and click **Go**. Select **SUMIFS** from the **Select a function** section and click **OK**.

3. In the **Sum_range** field select or enter **C5:C24**

4. In the **Criteria_range1** field select or enter **B5:B24**

5. In the **Criteria1** field enter **>10000**

6. In the **Criteria_range2** field select or enter **B5:B24**

7. In the **Criteria2** field enter **<20000**

8. Click **OK**.

Ex1_Q11.

1. Click **Employee Records** Worksheet and select cell **F7**

2. In the **Formulas** tab, locate the **Function Library** group, and select **Insert Function**. Search for and select **Countif**.

3. In **Range**, type or select **D7:D39**, and in **Criteria** type **Darwin**. Click **Ok**

Ex1_Q12.

1. Click the **Insert Worksheet** button. In the new worksheet, right click on **Sheet2** and click **Rename**. Type in **Office Expenses**. Click and drag the sheet to be right behind Office Records.

2. In the **Office Expenses** worksheet, in cell **A1** and enter <u>**Expenses**</u>. Click into cell **A2** In the **Data** tab, locate the **Data Tools** group, and select **Consolidate**.

3. In the **Consolidate** dialogue box, make sure that **SUM** is in the **Function** drop down. Click in the **Reference** area.

4. Select the **Office Records** worksheet. On the worksheet, select cells **A10:B23**. Click **Add**

5. Repeat step 4 for **E10:F23, A30:B43, E30:F43, A50:B63, E50:F63** and **A70:B83**

6. Under **Use Labels** in, check **Left Column**. Click **Ok**

Ex1_Q13

1. Select Cell **S12**. In the **Formulas** tab, locate the **Formula Auditing** group, and click **Evaluate Formula**.

2. The formula in the cell is located in the **Evaluation:** box. Click the **Evaluate** button. The underlined portion of the formula is evaluated each time that the evaluate button is clicked.

3. Click the **Evaluate** button twice. Notice that the Formula is subtracting **67895** from **50509**. The Total row should be adding, not subtracting. This is the error in the formula.

4. Click **Close** in the **Evaluate Formula** window.

5. Edit the Formula in cell **S12** to add the 3 cells instead of subtract.

Ex1_Q14.

1. In the **Employee Records** worksheet, select cell **F7**. In the **Formulas** tab, go to the **Function Library** group and click **Insert Function**.

2. In the **Insert Function** window, enter **VLOOKUP** and click **Go**. Select **VLOOKUP** from the **Select a function** section and click **OK**.

3. In the **Lookup_value** field enter <u>**Sam Tutu**</u>

4. In the **Table_array** field select or enter **A7:D39**

5. In the **Col_index_num** field enter **3**

6. In the Range_lookup field enter FALSE

7. Click **OK**.

Ex1_Q15.

1. Select the **Status Chart** worksheet. On this worksheet, select the chart

2. Click **Chart Tools Design Chart Layouts** group and click the **Quick Layout** dropdown, and select **Layout 1**

3. Click on **Chart Title** and type "**Employment History**"

4. In the **Chart Tools Design** tab, locate the **Chart Styles** group and click the drop down. Select **Style 9**

5. Right click the chart and click **Save as Template**. Navigate to the **PureSoftwareTemplate** folder in your documents folder, name the template **EmploymentChart** and click **Save**.

Ex1_Q16.

1. Click on the **Financial Data** chart, then click on the **Chart Elements** Flyout. Click the Flyout for **Trendline**, and click **More Options**.

2. Select the **2005** series, and click **OK**

3. In the **Format Trendline options**, select **Logarithmic** for the type. Under **Forecast**, type in **1.5** for **Forward**.

4. Select the **Other Data** chart, then click on the **Chart Elements** Flyout. Click the Flyout for **Trendline**, and click **Exponential**.

5. Select the **2005** series, and click **OK**

Ex1_Q17.

1. In the **Office Records** worksheet, select the title **Office Records**, which is cells **A4:G4**.

2. In the **Data** tab, **Data Tools** group, select the drop-down menu for **Data Validation**, and click on **Data Validation...**

3. Select the **Input Message** tab. Under **Input message:** type **Our office's income and expenses**. Leave all other values as they are.

4. Click **OK**

Ex1_Q18.

1. In the **Family Budget** worksheet, in the **Data** tab, go to the **Data Tools** group, click the **What-If Analysis** drop down and select **Scenario Manager**.

2. In the **Scenario Manager** window, click **Add**.

3. In the **Add Scenario** window, in the **Scenario name** enter **Wants** and in the changing cell select or enter **G22** and click **OK**.

4. In the **Scenario Values** window, enter **10000** and click **OK**.

5. Repeat steps 2 to 4, using the **scenario name Wishes** and the value **15000**

6. In the **Scenario Manager**, under the **Scenarios** section, highlight **Wants**, click **Show** and click **Close**.

Ex1_Q19.

1. Click the **New Sheet** button. In the new worksheet, right click on **Sheet2** and click **Rename**. Type in **Cut Costs**.

2. In the **Cut Costs** worksheet, click cell **A1**. In the **Data** tab, locate the **Data Tools** group, and select **Consolidate**.

3. In the **Consolidate** dialogue box, make sure that **Sum** is in the **Function** drop down. Click in the **Reference** area.

4. Select the **Family Budget** worksheet. On this worksheet, select cells **A6:D17**. Click **Add**

5. Repeat step 4 for **A21:D29**, **A33:D39**, and **A43:D49**

6. Under **Use Labels in**, check **Top Row** and **Left Column**. Click **Ok**

Ex1_Q20.

1. In the **Employee Records** worksheet, in the **Insert** tab, go to the **Tables** group, click the **PivotTable** drop down and select **PivotTable**.

2. In the **Select a table or range** field select **A6:D39**. In the **Choose where you...** section select **New Worksheet** and click **OK**.

3. In the new worksheet, in the **PivotTable Field List**, click and drag **Office** to the **Filter** group down below. Click and drag **Status** to the **Column** group, and drag **ID** and **First & Last Name** to the **Row** group.

4. Right click on the new worksheet, click **Rename** and enter **PivotTable**.

Ex1_Q21.

1. Select the Data in the **Employee Records** sheet, Cell range **A6:D39**. In the **Insert** tab, locate the **Charts** group, click the **PivotChart** dropdown, and select **PivotChart**. In the Create PivotChart window, click **OK**

2. In the **PivotChart Fields** box, Drag and Drop the **Status** field into the **Legend Fields (Series)** box.

3. Drag and Drop the **Office** field into the **Axis Fields (Categories)** box.

4. Drag and Drop the **ID** field into the **Values** box. This field will automatically change to **Sum of ID**.

5. Be sure the **First and Last Name** field is unchecked.

Ex1_Q22.

1. In the **Employee Records Table**, select anywhere in the PivotTable.

2. In the **Pivot Table Field List**, uncheck **Office**.

3. Drag **Status** from **Column Label** to **Row Label**, **First and Last Name** from **Reports Filter** to **Row Label**, and **Sum of ID** from **Values** to **Row Labels** (this will automatically convert to **ID**).

Ex1_Q23.

1. Select any part of the PivotTable. In the **PivotTable Tools/Analyze** tab, locate the **Filter** group, and click **Insert Slicer**.

2. In the **Insert Slicers** window, check the box for **Office**, and click **OK**

3. In the **Slicer Tools/Options** tab, locate the **Slicer** group, and enter <u>**Offices Shown**</u> in the **Slicer Caption** box.

4. In the **Slicer** window, select only **Sydney, Perth, and Melbourne**

Ex1_Q24.

1. In the **View** tab, locate the **Macros** group, click the **Macros** dropdown, and select **Record Macro**.

2. In the **Macro name:** box, enter <u>**Height**</u>. Leave the **Shortcut key** and **Description** boxes blank. In the **Store macro in:** box, select **This Workbook**. Click **OK**.

3. In the **Home** tab, locate the **Cells** group, click the **Format** dropdown, and select **Row Height**.

4. In the **Row Height** dialog box, enter <u>**30**</u>, and click **OK**.

5. In the **Home** tab, locate the **Font** group, and change the Font Size drop down to <u>**12**</u>.

6. In the **View** tab, locate the **Macros** group, select the **Macros** drop down, and click **Stop Recording**.

7. Select the range **A3:G9**. In the view tab, locate the **Macros** group, and click **Macros**. Run the macro **Height**.

Ex1_Q25.

1. In the **View** tab, locate the **Macros** group, click the **Macros** drop down, and select **Record Macro...**

2. In the **Macro name** field, enter <u>**Formatting**</u>. in the **Store macro in:** drop down, select **This Workbook**. Leave all other settings as the default, and click **OK**.

3. In the **Home** tab, locate the **number** group, and select **Currency** from the dropdown.

4. In the **Home** tab, locate the **Styles** group, and select the **Conditional Formatting** dropdown.

5. Select **Data Bars**, and click **Blue Data Bar** in the **Gradient** section.

6. In the **View** tab, locate the **Macros** group, click the **Macros** dropdown, and click **Stop Recording**.

7. Select the cell range **B4:G9**. In the **View** tab, locate the **Macros** group, click the **Macros** button, and **Run** the macro named **Formatting**.

Ex1_Q26.

If you do not have the Developer tab, you will need it:

1. Click on the **File** tab, select **Options**, and select the **Customize Ribbon** tab.

2. Make sure that **Developer** is checked in the **Main Tabs** section. Click **OK**

3. In the **Family Budget** worksheet, in the **Developer** tab, go to the **Controls** group, click the **Insert** drop down and select **Button (Form Control)**.

4. Click and drag over 1 to 2 open cells, in the **Assign Macro** window click **Set_Data_Bars** and click **OK**.

5. Click into the button to rename it, and enter **Set Data Bars**.

6. Click off the button, and then click the button to run it.

Ex1_Q27.

1. In the **Sales Orders** worksheet, in cell **H4**, right click on the **Spin Button** and click **Format Control**

2. In the **Format Control** window, go to the **Control** tab, in the **Minimum value** field enter **1** in the **Maximum value** field enter **100** and in the **Incremental change** field enter **1**.

3. Click **OK**.

Ex1_Q28.

If you do not have the Developer tab, you will need it:

1. Click on the **File** tab, select **Options**, and select the **Customize Ribbon** tab.

2. Make sure that **Developer** is checked in the **Main Tabs** section. Click **OK**

3. In the **Sale Orders** worksheet, click into the table, in the **Developer** tab, go to the **XML** group and click **Map Properties**.

4. In the **XML Map Properties** window, in the **Name** field enter **NewOrders**, under the **Data formatting and layout** section check the **Adjust column width** box.

5. Under the **When refreshing or importing data** section check the **Overwrite existing data with new data** radio button and click **OK**.

6. In the **Developer** tab, go to the **XML** group, and click **Export**.

7. Locate your exercise folder. In the file name enter **NewOrdersXML** and set the type to **XML Files (*.xml)** and click **Export**.

Ex1_Q29.

1. In the **File** tab, in the **Info** section, click on the drop down for **Properties** in the right hand column.

2. Click **Advanced Properties**, and choose the **Custom** tab

3. In **Name:** type **Completed**. In the drop down for **Type:** choose **Yes or No**. In **Value:** click **No**.

4. Click **Add**

5. Click **OK**

10.3 EXERCISE 2 QUESTIONS

Ex2_Q1.

Save the workbook as a template named **EmployeeReview** in any folder in your documents folder.

Notes:

_____

_____

_____

_____

_____

Ex2_Q2.

Require a password to open the current workbook using the password **ReviewHR9**

Notes:

_____

_____

_____

_____

_____

Ex2_Q3.

Protect the Employee Data worksheet with the password **ED2HR** (Leave all other settings as Default.)

Notes:

_____

_____

_____

_____

_____

Ex2_Q4.

Track all changes that have ever been made by any user on this shared document, only highlight changes when last saved. (Leave all other settings as Default.)

Ex2_Q5.

Merge the Ex2_Q1.xlsx worksheets with the current workbook.

Notes:

_____

_____

_____

_____

_____

Ex2_Q6.

In the **Business Trip Budget** worksheet, use the **Trace Precedents** for cell **G18** to determine the problem, and fix the formula.

Notes:

_____

_____

_____

_____

Ex2_Q7.

Configure Excel Formulas to have the R1C1 reference style and enable Error Checking using the colour Blue.

Notes:

_____

_____

_____

_____

_____

Ex2_Q8.

In the Yearly Timesheet worksheet, add watches to cells I4, K4 and M4.

Ex2_Q9.

Provide the option for Excel to highlight formulas that refer to empty cells in the **Error checking rules**.

Notes:

_____

_____

_____

_____

_____

Ex2_Q10.

In the **Startup Purchases** worksheet, using the **SUMIF** formula in the **Total Amount** Paid Off (**cell D22**), use the "**Paid?**" range data to compute the total of paid items.

Notes:

_____

_____

_____

_____

Ex2_Q11.

In the **Startup Expenses** worksheet, in cell **G11** do a **COUNTIF** for all the Totals below (**C11:C28**) to find out how many are greater than **125,000**

Notes:

_____

_____

_____

_____

_____

Ex2_Q12.

In the **Invoice Tracker** worksheet, under **Outstanding Invoices** (in cell **C23**) do a **COUNTIFS** for each client to find out how many still need to make payments on their invoices.

Notes:

_____

_____

_____

_____

_____

Ex2_Q13.

In the **Calculations** worksheet, in cell **F22** use the **COUNTIF** formula to find out how many employees are in the **R&D** Department.

Notes:

_____

_____

_____

_____

_____

Ex2_Q14.

In the **Calculations** worksheet, in cell **H18** use the **SUMIF** formula to find out how many **Total Sick Days** are in the **Finance Department**.

Notes:

_____

_____

_____

_____

Ex2_Q15.

In the **Business Trip Budget** worksheet, use the **Evaluate Formula** tool to correct the error in **G19** and simplify and correct the complex formula

Ex2_Q16.

In the **Dashboard** worksheet, create a **VLOOKUP** function in cell **N39** that finds the Bonus (Column 4) in the **Employee Data** worksheet for the Employee in **N35** in the **Dashboard** worksheet.

Notes:

_____

_____

_____

_____

Ex2_Q17.

In the **Dashboard** worksheet, add a **Linear Forecast** trendline to the **Number of Employees by Year** chart.

Notes:

_____

_____

_____

_____

Ex2_Q18.

In the **Dashboard** worksheet, fix the **Salary Distribution** chart to select the **Bonus** data from the **Employee Data** worksheet.

Notes:

_____

_____

_____

_____

_____

Ex2_Q19.

In the **Yearly Charts** worksheet, change the **January** chart to **Style 4**. Save the chart as a **chart template** with the name **TimecardChart** in the **any folder.**

Notes:

_____

_____

_____

_____

_____

Ex2_Q20.

Using the **Goal Seek Data Tool** set your **Trip Budget** for **Company (B23)** to **$15,000** to find out how many people are able to go on the business trip.

Notes:

_____

_____

_____

_____

_____

Ex2_Q21.

Create and show a scenario named <u>**Less**</u> that only gives **half** of what the **budget** had for **Entertainment** in cell **C15**. Create a Scenario Summary of the **Less Scenario.**

Notes:

_____

_____

_____

_____

_____

Ex2_Q22.

In the **Employee Data Pivot Chart** worksheet, insert slicers for **Full Name**, **Salary** and **Department**.

Notes:

_____

_____

_____

_____

_____

Ex2_Q23.

In the Invoice Tracker worksheet, insert a PivotTable beneath the data in cell E22 and shows the Invoice # and Outstanding data. Use the data in range B4:J17

Notes:

_____

_____

_____

_____

_____

Ex2_Q24.

In the **Employee Data Pivot Chart** worksheet, edit the **PivotChart**, and place the **Full Name** field into the **Axis (Categories)** group and the **Performance Score** into the **Values** group

Notes:

_____

_____

_____

_____

_____

Ex2_Q25.

In the **Invoice Tracker** worksheet, insert a **PivotTable** for cell range **B4:J17** into a new sheet that displays **Customer Name** and **Amount**. Accept all other defaults

Notes:

_____

_____

_____

_____

_____

Ex2_Q26.

In the **Invoice Tracker** worksheet, create a macro that sets the **Width** of all the columns to be **25**. Name the macro **ColumnWidth**, and store it in only this workbook (Leave all other settings as default settings.) and stop recording the Macro

Notes:

_____

_____

_____

_____

Ex2_Q27.

In the **Invoice Tracker** worksheet, assign the **Change_Colour** macro to the button **Change Table Colour** and click the button to run the Macro

Notes:

_____

_____

_____

_____

_____

Ex2_Q28.

In the **Startup Expenses** worksheet, create a **Spin Button** in cell **F8:F9** so that it changes the values in cell **F7** to numbers 1 - 100 in increments of 1. (Note: Accept all other default settings.)

Notes:

_____

_____

_____

_____

_____

Ex2_Q29.

In the **Dashboard** worksheet, link the **Form Control** above the **Employee Information** table to the **Employee Data** worksheet to the data under the <u>first column</u> heading and have the cell link be at **P34** on the **Dashboard** worksheet.

Notes:

_____

_____

_____

_____

10.4 EXERCISE 2: ANSWERS

Ex2_Q1.

1. In the **File** tab, click **Save As**.

2. In the **Save As** dialog window, locate your exercise folder in your documents folder, go to the **Save as type** drop down and select **Excel Template (.xltx)**.

3. Ensure that you are still in the exercise folder

4. In the **File name** field enter **<u>EmployeeReview</u>** and click **Save**.

Ex2_Q2.

1. **Click on File tab. On the Info tab**, select the **Protect Workbook** button and click **Encrypt with Password**.

2. In the dialog window enter the password **<u>ReviewHR9</u>** and click **OK**.

Ex2_Q3.

1. In the **Employee Data** worksheet, go to the **Review** tab, in the **Changes** group click **Protect S**heet.

2. In the **Protect Sheet** dialog window, in the **Password to unprotect sheet** field enter **<u>ED2HR</u>** and click **OK**.

Ex2_Q4.

1. In the **Employee Data** worksheet, in the **Review** tab, go to the **Changes** group, select the **Track Changes** drop down and click **Highlight Changes**.

2. In the **Highlight Changes** dialog window, click **Track changes while editing**. Set the **When** drop down to **Since I Last Saved**

3. Click the **Who** checkbox and set the drop down to **Everyone** and click **OK**.

Ex2_Q5.

1. In the **File** tab, click **Open**. In your exercise folder, open Ex2_Q1.xlsx workbook

2. In **Ex2_Q1.xlsx** right click on the **Invoice Tracker** worksheet, and click **Move or Copy**. Check the **Create a copy** checkbox.

3. In the **Move or Copy** dialog window, select the **To book** drop down and select **Ex2_Q5.xlsx**. In the **Before sheet** field select **Yearly Timesheet** and click **OK**.

Ex2_Q6.

1. In the **Business Trip Budget** worksheet, select cell **G18**.

2. In the **Formulas** tab, go to the **Formula Auditing** group and click **Trace Precedents**.

3. You will see that it is skipping cell G13. Select cells **G18**, in the **Home** tab, go to the **Editing** group and click the **AutoSum** drop down and select **Sum** and press Enter

Ex2_Q7.

1. In the **File** tab, click **Options**.

2. In the **Excel Options** window, select the **Formulas** tab, in the **Working with formulas** section check **R1C1 reference style**.

3. In the Error Checking section check **Enable background error checking**. In the colour drop down select **Blue** and click **OK**.

Ex2_Q8.

1. In the **Yearly Timesheet** worksheet, in the **Formulas** tab, go to the **Formula Auditing** group and click **Watch Window**.

2. In the **Watch Window** dialog window, click **Add Watch**.

3. Select cell **I4** and click **Add**.

4. Repeat steps 2 and 4 for cells **K4** and **M4**.

Ex2_Q9.

1. In the **File** tab, click **Options**.

2. In the **Excel Options** window, in the **Formulas** tab, go to the **Error checking rules** section and check **Formulas referring to empty cells** and click **OK**.

Ex2_Q10.

1. In the **Startup Purchases** worksheet, select cell **C22**. In the **Formulas** tab, go to the **Function Library** group and click **Insert Function**.

2. In the **Insert Function** window, search for **SUMIF** and click **GO**. Select **SUMIF** from the window below and click **OK**.

3. In the **Function Arguments** window, in the **Range** field select cells **D4:D20**.

4. In the **Criteria** field enter **Yes** and for the **Sum_range** field select the data in cells **C4:C20** and click **OK**.

Ex2_Q11.

1. In the **Startup Expenses** worksheet, select cell **G11**. In the **Formulas** tab, go to the **Function Library** group and click **Insert Function**.

2. In the **Insert Function** window, search for **COUNTIF** and click **GO**. Select **COUNTIF** from the window below and click **OK**.

3. In the **Function Arguments** window, in the **Range** field select cells **G15:G28**.

4. In the **Criteria** field enter **>125000** and click **OK**.

Ex2_Q12.

1. In the **Invoice Tracker** worksheet, select cells **C23:C26**. In the **Formulas** tab, go to the **Function Library** group and click **Insert Function**.

2. In the **Insert Function** window, in **the Search for Function** text box, enter **COUNTIFS** and click **GO**. Select **COUNTIF**S in the window below and click **OK**.

3. In the **Function Arguments** window, for the **Criteria_range1** field select cells **J4:J17** and in the **Criteria1** field enter **>0**.

4. In the **Criteria_range2** field select cells **E4:E17** and in the **Criteria2** field select cell **B23:B26** and click **OK**.

Ex2_Q13.

1. In the **Calculations** worksheet, select cell **F22**. In the **Formulas** tab, go to the **Function Library** and click **Insert Function**.

2. In the **Insert Function** window, search for **COUNTIF** and click **GO**. In the window select **COUNTIF** and click **OK**.

3. In the **Function Arguments** window, in the **Range** field select the data in the **Employee Data** worksheet from **F3:F98**. In the **Criteria** field select cell **A22 (R&D)** in the **Calculations** worksheet and click **OK**.

Ex2_Q14.

1. In thc **Calculations** worksheet, select cell **H18**. In the **Formulas** tab, go to the **Function Library** and click **Insert Function**.

2. In the **Insert Function** window, search for **SUMIF** and click **GO**. In the window select **SUMIF** and click **OK**.

3. In the **Function Arguments** window, in the **Range** field select the data in the **Employee Data** worksheet from cells **F3:F98**. In the **Criteria** field select cell **A18** in the **Calculations** worksheet, in the **Sum range** field select data from the **Employee Data** worksheet from cells **G3:G98** and click **OK**.

Ex2_Q15.

1. In the **Business Trip Budget** worksheet, select cell **G19**, in the **Formulas** tab, go to the **Formula Auditing** group and click **Evaluate Formula**.

2. In the **Evaluate Formula** window, click **Evaluate** to go through the steps of the formula until it returns to the first step, then click **Close**. (Look closely at what the formula is doing and how to correct it.)

3. In cell **G19** enter the formula **=B4-G18**.

Ex2_Q16.

1. In the **Dashboard** worksheet, select cell **N39**. In the **Formulas** tab, go to the **Function Library** and click **Insert Function**.

2. In the **Insert Function** window, search for **VLOOKUP** and click **GO**. In the window select **VLOOKUP** and click **OK**.

3. In the **Function Arguments** window, in the **Lookup_value** field select the data in the cell **N35**.

4. In the **Table_array** field select the data in the Employee Data worksheet cell **A3:H98**.

5. In the **Col_index_num** enter **4**. In the Range_lookup, enter **FALSE** and click **OK**.

Ex2_Q17.

1. In the **Dashboard** worksheet, select the **Number of Employees by Year** chart.

2. Click the **chart elements** button that appears at the top right of the chart. Select the **Trendline** drop down and click **linear forecast**.

Ex2_Q18.

1. In the **Dashboard** worksheet, select the **Salary Distribution** chart.

2. In the **Design** tab, go to the **Data** group and click **Select Data**.

3. In the **Select Data Source** window, select the data from **D3:D98** and click **OK**.

Ex2_Q19.

1. In the **Yearly Charts** worksheet, select the **January** chart. In the **Design** tab, go to the **Chart Styles** group and select **Style 4**.

2. Right click in the Yearly Charts worksheets and select the **Save As Template**

3. In the **Save Chart Template** window, locate the GTotalTemplates folder located in your documents folder. In the **File name** field enter **TimecardChart** and click **Save**.

Ex2_Q20.

1. In the **Business Trip Budget** worksheet, select cell **B23**. In the **Data** tab, go to the **Forecast** group, select the **What-If Analysis** drop down and click **Goal Seek**.

2. In the **Goal Seek** window, set the Set cell field as **B23**, set the To value field to 15000 and the By changing cell field to **B22** and click **OK** twice.

Ex2_Q21.

1. In the **Data** tab, go to the **Data Tools** group, select the **What-If Analysis** drop down and click **Scenario Manager**.

2. In the **Scenario Manager** window, click **Add**. In the **Scenario name** field enter **Less**. Set the Changing cells to **C15** and click **OK**.

3. In the Scenario Values window set the value to **65** and click **OK**.

4. Select the Result cells (**G18:G19**)

5. In the **Scenario Manager**, highlight the **Less** Scenario and click **Summary**

6. In the **Scenario Summary** window click **OK**

Ex2_Q22.

1. In the **Employee Data Pivot Chart** worksheet, highlight the **PivotTable**.

2. Click the Insert tab.

3. In the **Filter** group click **Slicer**

4. In the **Insert Slicers** window, click **Full Name**, **Salary** and **Department** and click **OK**.

Ex2_Q23.

1. In the **Invoice Tracker** worksheet, in the **Insert** tab, locate the **Tables** group, and click **PivotTable**

2. In the Create **PivotTable** window, for **select a table or range** select the cells **B4:J17** and under the **Choose where...** section click Existing Worksheet. In the Location field select **E22** and click **OK**.

3. Highlight the **PivotTable** and in the **PivotTable Fields** window select **Invoice #** and **Outstanding**.

Ex2_Q24.

1. In the **Employee Data Pivot Chart** worksheet, highlight the **PivotChart**.

2. In the **PivotChart Fields** window, drag **Full Name** to the **Axis (Categories)** group below and the **Performance Score** to the **Values** group below.

Ex2_Q25.

In the **Invoice Tracker** worksheet, insert a **PivotTable** for cell range **B4:J17** into a new sheet that displays **Customer Name** and **Amount**. Accept all other defaults

1. In the **Invoice Tracker** worksheet select the, in the **Insert** tab, go to the **Tables** group, select the **PivotTable** drop down and click **PivotTable**.

2. In the **Create PivotTable** window, in the select a table or range select the cells **B4:J17** and under the Choose where... section click **New Worksheet** and click **OK**.

3. Highlight the PivotTable and in the **PivotTable Field List** window select **Customer Name** and **Amount**.

Ex2_Q26.

1. In the **Invoice Tracker** worksheet, in the **Developer** tab, go to the **Code** group, and click **Record Macro**.

2. In the **Record Macro** dialog window in the **Macro name** field enter **ColumnWidth** and click **OK**.

3. Select columns B to J. Right-click on any of the column's while the columns are selected and click **Column Width**.

4. In the **Column Width** dialog window, enter 25 and click **OK**.

5. In the **Developer** tab, go to the **Code** group and click **Stop Recording**.

Ex2_Q27.

1. In the **Invoice Tracker** worksheet, right click on the **Change Table Colour** button below the table and click **Assign Macro..**

2. In the **Assign Macro** dialog window, select the **Change Colour** macro from the list and click **OK**. Click out of the **Change Table Colour** button, so it is no longer selected.

3. Click the **Change Table Colour** button.

Ex2_Q28.

1. In the **Startup Expenses** worksheet, in the **Developer** tab, go to the **Controls** group, in the **Insert** dropdown select **Spin Button**.

2. Draw the Spin Button in top of cell **F8** to the bottom right of **F9**. Right click on the Spin Button and select **Format Control**.

3. In the **Format Control** dialog window set the **Minimum value** to 1 and **Maximum value** to 100. Set the Cell link to cell F7 and click **OK**.

Ex2_Q29.

1. In the **Dashboard** worksheet, right click on the **Form Control** above the **Employee Information** table and click **Format Control**.

2. In the **Format Object** dialog window, in the **Control** tab, enter your cursor into the **Input Range** field and select the **Employee Data** worksheet, highlight all the data from cell **A3:A98**.

3. In the **Format Object** dialog window, click into the **Cell link** field and in the **Dashboard** worksheet select cell **P34** and click **OK**.

10.5 EXERCISE 3: QUESTIONS & ANSWERS

Ex3_Q1.

Protect the structure of the workbook.

1. Choose **Review** ➜ **Changes** group ➜ **Protect Workbook.** In the Change group, click **Protect Workbook**

2. In the Protect Workbook dialog box, select the **Structure** option

3. (Optional) Provide a password.

Notes:

To unprotect the workbook, repeat the process and untick the **Structure** option and click **Cancel.**

_____

_____

_____

_____

_____

Ex3_Q2.

Make the **Loan Payment** worksheet "VeryHidden" so that you cannot unhide it in the normal way.

1. Activate the **Loan Payment** worksheet Chose **Developer Controls Properties**

2. In the **Properties** dialog box, select the Visible property and choose **2-SheetVeryHidden**.

Notes:

To unhide a sheet that is VeryHidden, Press Alt-F11 to activate the Visual Basic editor. Locate the workbook in the Projects window and select the name of the sheet that is VeryHidden. Press F4 to display the Properties dialog box, then change the **Visible** property back to 1-SheetVisible.

_____

_____

_____

_____

• You cannot hide the last and only sheet in a workbook.

Ex3_Q3.

On the **Business Trip Budget** worksheet, provide a **Watch Window** for cells **G18** and **G19.**

1. On the **Business Trip Budget** worksheet, Click the **Formula** tab

2. In the **Formula Auditing** group click **Watch Window**

3. Select cells **G18** and **G19**

4. On the **Watch Window** dialog box, click **Add Watch.**

5. On the **Add Watch** dialog box click the **Add** button.

Notes:

_____

_____

_____

_____

_____

Ex3_Q4.

Apply the **Accounting** formatting to cells **B4:F8** in all the four worksheets in a **group mode** (i.e. apply the format to all the sheets at once, not one by one).

1. Activate the first (**Totals**) sheet

2. Select the range **B4:F8**

3. Press **Shift** and click the **Manufacture** sheet tab (the last sheet)

4. Click the **Home** tab and then click the **Number** group dialog launcher

5. Select **Accounting** and click **OK**

6. Right-click any of the grouped sheets and select **Ungroup sheets**

Ex3_Q5.

On the **Totals** worksheet, change the shape of the rectangular comments box in cell **F8** to a different shape of your choice. Hint: First you need to add a command to the Quick Access toolbar:

1. Right-click on the Quick Access toolbar and choose **Customize Quick Access Toolbar**

2. From the **Choose Command from** drop-down list, select **Drawing Tools | Format Tab**

3. From the list on the left, select **Change Shape**, and then click **Add**, then click **OK.**

4. Make the comment box visible.

5. Press the **Ctrl** key and click the rectangular **Comment** box.

6. Click the **Change Shape** button on the **Quick Access** toolbar and choose a new shape for the comment.

Ex3_Q6

Print the **Totals** worksheet together with its comments. The comments should appear on a separate page at the end of the sheet printout.

1. Click the dialog box launcher (⊠) in the **Page Layout → Page Setup group**.

2. In the **Page Setup** dialog box, click the **Sheet** tab.

3. In the **Comments** textbox select **At End of Sheet**, and click **OK.**

Ex3_Q7.

In the **House Sales** worksheet sort the table data by: **Agent** (**A-Z**), then by **Area** (**Z-A**) and finally by **List Price (smallest to largest)**

1. Click any cell within the data cells.

2. In the **Editing** group on the **Home** tab, click on the **Sort & Filter** tab.

3. Select **Custom Sort** to open the **Custom Sort** dialog box

4. In the **Sort by** drop-down list select **Agent,** In the **Sort On** drop-down, select **Value,** and in **the Order** drop-down select **A-Z**. Click **Add Level.**

5. In the **Sort by** drop-down list select **Area,** In the **Sort On** drop-down, select **Value,** and in **the Order** drop-down select **Z-A**. Click **Add Level.**

6. In the **Sort by** drop-down list select **List Price,** In the **Sort On** drop-down, select **Value,** and in **the Order** drop-down select **Smallest to Largest**.

Notes:

_____

_____

_____

_____

_____

Ex3_Q8.

In the **House Sales** worksheet, using Slicers, filter the table data to show only records for the Agent called **Adams** in the **Central** Area.

1. Click any cell in the table.

2. In the **Filters** group on the **Insert** tab, click **Slicer.**

3. Check the **Agent** and **Area** boxes and click **OK**

4. On the **Agent** slicer click **Adams**, and click **Central** on the **Area** slicer

Notes:

_____

_____

_____

_____

_____

1. To remove the filter click on the **Clear Filter** icon or use **Alt + C**

2. To delete the slicer, activate it and press **Delete**

Ex3_Q9.

In addition to Excel's **XLStart** folder, use the "**C:\Pure Training**" folder, as an alternate Startup folder.

1. Choose **File Options** and select the **Advanced** tab.

2. Scroll down to the **General** section and enter a new folder name (in this case "**C:\Pure Training**") in the **At Startup, open all files in** textbox.

Notes:

Excel will attempt to open all files (e.g. *.docx) that are stored in this folder. Make sure only the Excel file that you wish to open at startup is stored in the folder

_____

_____

_____

_____

_____

Ex3_Q10.

Protect only the formula cells on Sheet1 (Leave nonformula cells unprotected).

1. Choose **Home** → **Editing** group → **Find & Select** → **Go to Special**

2. Select **Constants** and click **OK**. All nonformula cells are selected

3. Press **Ctrl + 1** to open the **Format Cell** dialog box

4. Select the **Protection** tab

5. Remove the check mark from the **Locked** checkbox, and click **Ok**.

6. Choose **Review Changes** Protect Sheet

7. (Optional) Specify a password and click **OK**

Notes:

_____

_____

_____

_____

_____

Ex3_Q11.

In Sheet1 print only range **A11:H23 (yellow highlight)**.

1. In **Sheet1**, select range **A11:H23**.

2. On the Ribbon click **File Print**.

3. In the Print dialog box, under **Settings**, click the drop-down arrow for the **Print Active Sheets** option and click the **Print Selection** option.

Notes:

_____

_____

_____

_____

_____

Ex3_Q12.

On the Customer Contact Details sheet, insert **FIRST PAGE HEADER** in the first page header only. Insert **FIRST PAGE FOOTER** in the first page footer only. Insert **ODD PAGE HEADER** in all odd page headers and **ODD PAGE FOOTER** in all odd page footers. Insert **EVEN PAGE HEADER** in all even page headers, then insert **EVEN PAGE FOOTER** in all even page footers.

1. On the Ribbon, click **View → Workbook View → Page Layout**

2. Click in the box containing the text "**Add Header**"

3. Click the **DESIGN** tab under **Header & Footer Tools**.

4. In the **Options** group, check the check boxes for **Different First Page** and **Different Odd and Even Pages.**

5. Type **FIRST PAGE HEADER** in the header box for the first page.

6. Type **FIRST PAGE FOOTER** in the footer box for the first page.

Notes:

_____

_____

_____

_____

_____

Ex3_Q13.

On the **Customer Contact Details** worksheet, configure **Page Setup** for "**Landscape**" orientation and set **Page Size** to **B5**. Apply the configuration to **Sheet1** worksheet.

1. Activate the **Customer Contact Details** worksheet (source).

2. Select the target sheet (the new sheet). Do a Ctrl + click to activate both sheets.

3. Click the dialog box launcher in the lower right corner of the **Page Layout Page Setup** group.

4. When the dialog box appears, click **OK** and close it.

5. Ungroup the sheet by right-clicking any selected sheet and choosing **Ungroup Sheets** from the shortcut menu.

Notes:

_____

_____

_____

_____

_____

Ex3_Q14.

Set up the **Customer Contact Details** sheet so that the SmartArt Graphic (with the text "**Do not Print**") does not print when the worksheet is printed.

1. Right-click the object and choose **Format Shape**

2. In the **Format** dialog box, click the **Size & Properties** icon

3. Expand the **Properties** section of the dialog box

4. Remove the check mark for **Print Object**

Notes:

_____

_____

_____

_____

_____

Ex3_Q15.

Create a custom view named "**Customer Contact Details No1**" for the **Customer Contact Details** sheet. Accept all default options

1. Choose **View Workbook View Custom Views**. The Custom Views dialog box appears.

2. Click the Add button.

3. On the Add View dialog box type **Customer Contact Details No1** in the **Name** box.

Notes:

_____

_____

_____

_____

_____

1. You will normally create different views (with different settings for different requirements) for the same worksheet.

2. The Custom View command is disabled if ANY sheet in the workbook has a table.

3. When you are ready to print, just select the appropriate view (e.g. one with correct print margins etc.)

Ex3_Q16.

The data in range **B3:D14** is a table called **Table1**. Without resorting to using any Excel formula, show the **sum** of the **Projected** column and the **Standard Deviation** of the data in the **Actual** column (include a **Total** row in the table).

1. Click any cell in the table (**Table1**).

2. Under **Table Tools**, click **Design.**

3. In the **Table Style Options** group, put a check mark in the **Total Row** check box.

4. Click the cell in the **Total** row in the Projected column (cell **C15**). In the drop-down list select **SUM.**

5. Click the cell in the **Total** row in the **Actual** column (cell **D15**). In the drop-down list select **StdDev.**

Notes:

_____

_____

_____

_____

_____

Ex3_Q17.

On the **Accounts** sheet in cell **B17**, use the **DSUM** function to calculate the total account balance for all **Open** accounts that have rates greater than 2 percent.

	A	B	C	D
1				
2	Bank	Rate	Balance	Status
3		>0.02		Open

1. Create a table as shown above on the **Account** sheet

2. Create this formula in cell **B17**: **=DSUM (A5:D15,"Balance", A2:D3)**

Notes:

1. DSUM syntax: DSUM (Database, Field, Criteria range)

2. Database (range) is: A5:D15

3. Target field for calculation is: "Balance"

4. Criteria range is: A2:D3 (this range can be placed anywhere on the sheet)

Ex3_Q18.

In the **Data** worksheet, use the **ROW** and **INDIRECT** functions to calculate the total of the <u>five largest values</u> in range **A1:A25**.

1. Select any empty cell in the data sheet

2. Use this formula: **={SUM(LARGE(A1:A25, ROW(INDIRECT("1:5"))))}**

Notes:

1. DO NOT type the curly brackets ({})

2. After typing the formula, press Shift+Ctrl+ENTER (DO NOT press only the ENTER key)

3. The combination of the ROW and INDIRECT functions produces the array {1,2,3,4,5}

4. So in effect the formula becomes: SUM(LARGE (A1:A25,{1,2,3,4,5}))

5. Read on the LARGE, ROW and INDIRECT functions

Ex3_Q19.

In cell **B3** on the **Tax Rate** sheet, use the **VLOOKUP** function to retrieve the value of the **Tax Rate** for an income of **$55,000**.

1. In cell **B3** insert this formula: **=VLOOKUP(55000,D2:F7,3)**

Notes:

_____

_____

_____

_____

_____

1. Syntax: VLOOKUP (lookup_value, table_array, col_index_num [,range_lookup]

2. If an exact match is not found in the first column of the lookup table, VLOOKUP uses the next largest value that is less than the lookup value.

Ex3_Q20.

Make the necessary adjustment on the **Chart** worksheet so that only **Chart1** and the data should appear when the sheet is printed. **Chart2** should not be printed.

1. Access the **Format Chart Area** task pane for **Chart2** (Double-click the **Chart Area** for **Chart2**).

2. Select the **Property & Size** icon.

3. Expand the **Properties** section and clear the **Print** check box.

Notes:

_____

_____

_____

_____

_____

Ex3_Q21.

On **Sheet1**, hide (**NOT** delete) the data series for **Precipitation** from the **Weather Summary** chart.

1. Activate the chart and click **Chart Filter** button on the right.

2. Remove the check mark from the data series for **Precipitation**

Notes:

_____

_____

_____

_____

_____

Ex3_Q22.

On the **Combo Chart** sheet, create a **combination chart** for the two data series (**Column chart** for the **Avg. Temp** series and **Line chart** for the **Precipitation** series).

Make the Precipitation data series the Secondary Axis.

1. Select any cell in the data area

2. Choose **Insert** Charts **Recommended Charts**.

3. Select the **All Charts** tab.

4. In the list of chart types, click **Combo**.

5. For the **Avg. Temp** series, specify **Clustered Column** as the chart type

6. For the **Precipitation** series, specify **Line** as the chart type and click the **Secondary Axis** check box.

7. Click **OK** to insert the chart

Notes:

_____

_____

_____

_____

_____

Ex3_Q23.

On the **nonnumeric** sheet, format only the text entries (cells containing text) **bold.** All cells containing numbers should not be formatted.

1. Select the range **A1:B10** and ensure that cell **A1** is the active cell.

2. Choose **Home Styles Conditional Formatting New Rule**.

3. Click the **Use Formula to Determine Which Cells to Format** rule type.

4. Enter the following formula in the Formula box: **=ISTEXT(A1).**

5. Click the **Format** button.

6. From the **Font** tab, select **Bold.**

7. Click **OK** to return to the **New Formatting Rule** dialog box

8. Click **OK** to close the New **Formatting Rule** dialog box

Notes:

1. If the formula that is entered into the conditional formatting dialog box contains a cell reference, that reference is considered a *relative reference*, based on the upper-left cell in the selected range.

_____

_____

_____

_____

_____

Ex3_Q24.

On the **Custom Format** sheet, using the **Today ()** function enter today's date in cell **A1** in the format **"mm/dd/yyyy"** or **"dd/mm/yyyy"**. Format the cell to read, for example, **August 03, 2015 (Monday)** in **Red** text

Notes:

_____

_____

_____

_____

1. In cell **A1** enter: **=Today()**

2. Click the dialog box launcher of the **Home Font** tab

3. Click the **Number** tab. In the **Category** list select the **Custom** option

4. In the **Type** box enter the following format: **[RED]mmmm dd, yyyy (dddd)**

** **Open the Custom Format Example sheet to see examples of custom formatting.**

Ex3_Q25.

Apply the **General** format as the <u>default</u> format for the workbook.

Notes:

_____

_____

_____

_____

_____

1. Select the **Home** tab **Style Cell Style** drop-down.

2. Right-click the **Normal** style **Modify**. Select the **General** format. Click **OK.**

Ex3_Q26.

On the **West Companies** sheet, modify the existing **Conditional Formatting** rule to remove the values from then **2015 Sales** column and show only the data bars.

Notes:

_____

_____

_____

_____

_____

1. Click **Home Styles Conditional Formatting Manage Rules**

2. On the **Show format rule for** drop-down box select "**This Worksheet**"

3. Activate the **Data Bar** rule and click **Edit Rule…**

4. Click the **Show bar only** text box

Ex3_Q27.

On the **Feb_Humidity** sheet, highlight (using Red colour) all humidity values that are <u>less</u> than their corresponding **Jan_Humidity** values.

1. Select the humidity values on the **Feb Humidity** sheet (**B2:H21**).

2. Click **Home Styles Conditional Formatting** drop-down

3. Select the **Manage Rules…** option

4. On the **Conditional Formatting Rules Manager** dialog box, click the **New Rule** tab.

5. Select the **Use a formula to determine which cells to format** option.

6. In the **Format values where this formula is true** text box, type the following formula: **B2< Jan_Humidity!B2**

7. Click the Format tab and in the Colour drop-down select Red

Note: If you select the cells for the formula instead of typing them in, excel by default will add the $ signs for absolute references. In that case manually delete the $ signs

Ex3_Q28.

In the **Auto Fill** sheet, Create an **Auto Fill** using the cities in cells **A3:A11**. Type **Sydney** in cell **C3** and drag the **Fill handler** to auto-fill cells **C4:C11** with the rest of the cities (just as in cells **A3:A11**).

Notes:

_____

_____

_____

_____

_____

1. Click **File Options Advanced**.

2. Scroll down and click the **Edit Custom List** button.

3. In the **List entries** list box enter the cities (**Sydney…Newcastle**), separated by commas (,).

4. Click **Add** and then click **OK.**

5. In the **Auto Fill** sheet, select cell **C3**, enter **Sydney.**

6. Drag down to fill the cells.

Ex3_Q29.

In the Status Chart worksheet, change the chart layout to Layout 1, change the chart title to Employment History and change the chart style to Style 9. Save the chart as a chart template to the PureSoftwareTemplate folder in your documents folder and with the name EmploymentChart

Notes:

_____

_____

_____

_____

_____

1. Select the Status Chart worksheet. On this worksheet, select the chart

2. Click Chart Tools Design Chart Layouts group and click the Quick Layout dropdown, and select Layout 1

3. Click on Chart Title and type "Employment History"

4. In the Chart Tools Design tab, locate the Chart Styles group and click the drop down. Select Style 9

5. Right click the chart and click Save as Template. Navigate to the PureSoftwareTemplate folder in your documents folder, name the template EmploymentChart and click Save.

Ex3_Q30.

Using a <u>named formula</u> called "**Address**", the **INDEX** function and the **MATCH** function, provide a means to retrieve the address into cell **G3** for a name entered in cell **G1**. Use one of the names in the **A3:A10** range. Ensure that no error message is shown if the name does not exist in the list. If the name does not exist, the address cell (**G3**) must be blank.

1. Click **Formula → Define Names → Define Name**

2. In the **New Name** dialog box, enter "**Address**" into the **Name** textbox

3. In the "**Refers to:**" textbox, enter:

=IFERROR (INDEX($A$3:$B$10, MATCH($G$1,$A$3:$A$10,0),2),"")

1. Click **OK**

2. In cell **G3** enter the formula **"=Address"**

10.6 EXERCISE 4: QUESTIONS & ANSWERS

Ex4_Q1.

Use the data in cells **A3:A10** as a drop-down list for cell **G1**. Then in cell **G3**, write a **VLOOKUP** function to show the address of a name selected from the drop-down list in cell **G1**.

1. Click in cell **G1**.

2. Click **Data Data Tools**. Click the drop-down arrow for the **Data Validation** tab.

3. In the **Data validation** dialog box, in the **Allow:** drop-down, select **List**

4. Click in the **Source** textbox and highlight cells **A3:A10**. Click **OK.**

5. Enter this formula in cell **G3**: **"=VLOOKUP(G1, A3:B10, 2, FALSE)"**

Ex4_Q2.

** Use <u>ONLY</u> The INDEX, MATCH, VLOOKUP and DOLLAR functions for the following question:

The "**Dollar, Match, VLOOKUP & Index**" Worksheet has 3 option buttons for mailing types and costs. Cell **B2** is a linked cell for the option buttons. Using the data area (range **A7:C9**), construct a formula that will display the following information in cell **A12**:

a.) When you select **Option 1** (**Air Mail**), cell **A12** should read: "**Cost of Using Air Mail is $124.78**"

b.) When you select **Option 2** (**Courier**), cell **A12** should read: "**Cost of Using Courier is $450**"

c.) When you select **Option 3** (**Surface Mail**) cell **A12** should read: "**Cost of Using Surface Mail is $99.56**"

In cell A12 enter the following formula:

="Cost of Using " & INDEX(A7:C9, MATCH ($B$2,$B$7:$B$9,0),1) & " is " & DOLLAR(VLOOKUP(B2,B7:C9,2,FALSE))

Ex4_Q3.

On the **Chart** worksheet, create an **Exponential Trendline** based on the **YR2010** data series. Include a future trend of 2.5.

1. Click the chart.

2. Click the **Chart Element** icon that appears to the right of the chart

3. From the list of chart elements click the arrow to the right of "**Trendline**"

4. Click "**More Options**"

5. On the **Add a Trendline based on Series**: dialog box, select **YR2010** and click **OK**

6. On the "**Format Trendline**" task pane, click "**Trendline Options**"

7. Select the "**Exponential**" option

8. In the "**Forecast**" section, enter 2.5 in the "**Forward**" textbox

9. Close the task pane

Ex4_Q4.

In the **Consolidation** worksheet, in cell **A2,** consolidate the Expenses data in the "**Office Records**" sheet using the following ranges: **A10:B23**; **E10:F23**; **A30:B43**; **E30:F43**; **A50:B63**; **E50:F63** and **A70:B83**. Use the **SUM** function for the consolidation and add labels from the left column.

1. Select cell **A2** in the **Consolidation** worksheet.

2. **Data → Data Tools** group → **Consolidate. Ensure that the cursor is in the "Reference" textbox.**

3. On the **Office Records** worksheet, select range **A10:B23**

4. Click **Add** in the consolidate dialog box

5. Repeat steps **3** and **4** for **E10:F23**; **A30:B43**; **E30:F43**; **A50:B63**; **E50:F63** and **A70:B83**

6. In the **Consolidate** dialog box, in the "**Use label in**" section, select the "**Left column**" checkbox.

7. On the **Consolidate** dialog box click **OK.**

Ex4_Q5.

The **Choose Function** worksheet has 3 option buttons for mailing types and costs. Cell **B2** is a linked cell for the option buttons. Using the data in cells **A7:C9** and the linked cell, use the CHOOSE function to construct a formula that will display the following information in cell **A12:**

a.) When you select **Option 1 (Air Mail)**, cell **A12** should read: "**Cost of Using Air Mail is $124.78**"

b.) When you select **Option 2 (Courier)**, cell **A12** should read: "**Cost of Using Courier is $450**"

c.) When you select **Option 3 (Surface Mail)** cell **A12** should read: "**Cost of Using Surface Mail is $99.56**"

In cell **A12** type the following formula:

=”The Cost of Using “ & CHOOSE (B2, A7, A8, A9) & “ is “ & DOLLAR (CHOOSE (B2, C7, C8, C9))

Hint:

Use the CHOOSE function twice.

Ex4_Q6

In the **Advanced Filter** worksheet, use range **A3:G4** as the **Criteria Range** to filter the data (**A5:G21**). The filtered data should display:

a.) Advanced Computers accounts with overdue invoices (Days Overdue > 0) AND

b.) Pure Software accounts with overdue invoices > $2,000

The filtered information should be similar to the following:

Account Name	Account Number	Invoice Number	Invoice Amount	Due Date	Date Paid	Days Overdue
Advanced Computers	10-0009	117321	$3,983.66	30/07/2015		12
Advanced Computers	10-0009	117327	$844.34	12/07/2015		30
Pure Software	01-0047	678234	$3,426.62	24/08/2015		23
Pure Software	01-0049	902341	$8,568.96	7/06/2015		7
Pure Software	01-0050	902135	$3,956.95	8/07/2015		2

1. In cell **A3** enter “**Pure Software**”

2. In cell **A4** enter “**Advanced Computers**”

3. In cell **D3** enter “**>2000**”

4. In cell **G3** enter “**>0**”

5. In cell **G4** enter “**>0**”

6. Click **Data Sort & Filter Advanced**

7. On the **Advanced Filter** dialog box:

    a.) In the List Range text box, select range A5:G21

    b.) In the Criteria Range text box, select range A2:G4 and click OK

Ex4_Q7.

In the **Database Function** worksheet, range **A7:G22** is a table (database) named “**Invoice**”. Using range

A2:A3 as **Criteria Range,** with **A3** as the criteria cell, in cell G3 compute the average invoice amount for the "**Pure Software**" account. Use the **DAVERAGE** function and a table specifier.

1. In cell **A2** enter "**Account Name**"

2. In cell **A3** enter "**Pure Software**"

3. In cell **G3** enter the following formula:

=DAVERAGE(Invoice[#All],"Invoice Amount", A2:A3)

Ex4_Q8.

Using the Pivot Table worksheet, create the Pivot Table shown below:

Order Date	(All)		
Sum of Amount	**Column Labels**		
Row Labels	**ALTA**	**BC**	**Grand Total**
Brown	114326.26		114326.26
Davidson	147473.66		147473.66
Fletcher		61102.12	61102.12
Johnson	91391.5		91391.5
King		89869.13	89869.13
Lee		64081.69	64081.69
McDonald	161100.13		161100.13
Peterson	208528.98		208528.98
Thompson		66868.36	66868.36
Grand Total	**722820.53**	**281921.3**	**1004741.83**

1. **Click any cell within the data**

2. **Click Insert PivotTable**

3. **In the Create PivotTable dialog box, choose the "Select a table or range option"**

4. **In the "Table/Range" textbox enter (or highlight) the data source (A1:E651)**

5. **Select the "New Worksheet" option for the location of the PivotTable and click OK.**

6. **In the PivotTable Fields task pane, drag the fields into the areas as follows:**

    a.) Column: Province field

    b.) Row: Salesperson fields

    c.) Value: Amount field

    d.) Filter: Order Date

Ex4_Q9.

Use the **PivotTable** worksheet to compute the relative importance of each promotional method with respect to the items on promotion.

1. Right-click any cell inside the data field

2. Select "**Summarize Values By**:" and click the **SUM** calculation

3. Right-click any cell inside the data field

4. Select **Show Values As**, Index.

Note: The higher the index value, the more important the cell is in the overall results.

Ex4_Q10.

The **Calculated Column** worksheet contains a Pivot Table. Create a calculated column in the Pivot Table called "**Difference**" that computes the difference between the monthly **Actual** and **Projected** values (**Actual – Projected**).

1. Click any cell in the Pivot Table data area

2. Select **Analyze Calculation**s **Fields, Items, & Sets** drop-down

3. In the Name text box enter "**Difference**"

4. In the Formula text box enter "**=Actual – Projected**"

5. Click Add. Click **OK**

Ex4_Q11.

On the **Product Margin** worksheet, use the appropriate **What-If Analysis** tool and the data on the sheet to determine at what price an item must be sold (**Unit Price**) to obtain a **Margin** of **30 percent**.

Note: Enter 30 percent as 0.3

1. **Data → Data Tools → What-If Analysis**

2. On the Drop-down, select **Goal Seek**…and enter the information as shown below

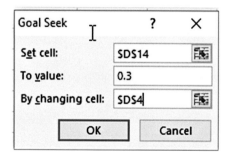

You should obtain a margin of 29.93% at a unit price of appro. $37.18.

Ex4_Q12.

In the "**Computers**" worksheet, in cell **F14**, write a formula to compute the sum of the total cost for **Division 3** computers. Utilize the existing "**Computers**" range name (called "**Parts**") in your formula.

In cell F14, enter the following formula:

=SUMIF(Computers[Division], "=3", Computers[Total Cost])

Ex4_Q13.

Exercise folder, there is a workbook called "**Copysheet.xlxs**. Copy the worksheet called "**CopyMe**" into the current workbook. Place it before "**Sheet1**"

1. In the current workbook, click **File Open**

2. Open the **Copysheet.xlxs** in your exercise folder

3. Right-click "**CopyMe**" worksheet tab and select "**Move or Copy**"

4. In the **To book**: dropdown, select **Ex4_Q14** workbook.

5. In the Before sheet list, select "**Sheet1**"

6. Tick the **Create a copy** checkbox and click **OK**

Ex4_Q14.

In the **Customer Contact Details** sheet, configure print options to print column headers (row 6) on every printout page.

1. Choose **Page Layout Page Setup Print Titles**.

2. Activate the "**In the Rows to repeat at top:**" text box in the **Sheet** tab, .

3. Highlight row 6 (the header row) and click **OK**.

Ex4_Q15.

Format the "**Headers & Footers**" worksheet so that on the printout, page headers will be printed as follows:

Left section:	Current Date
Middle section:	"Pure Software Training"
Right section:	Page x of y

1. Click **View Workbook Views Page Layout.**

2. On the **Page Layout** view of the worksheet, activate the page header by clicking at the top.

3. In the left box of the page header, enter **&[Date].**

4. In the centre box of the page header, enter "**Pure Software Training && Consulting**".

5. In the right box of the page header, enter **Page &[Page] of &[Pages].**

6. Click anywhere on the sheet outside of the page header.

Ex4_Q16.

On the "**Headers & Footers**" sheet, apply the following <u>**Page Setup**</u> settings:

Bottom margin **= 0**; Page Centre= **Horizontally & Vertically**;

Page Orientation = **Landscape**; Paper Size = **B5**.

<u>**Copy**</u> these settings to the **FormatMe1** and **FormatMe2** sheets

1. **Activate the "Header & Footer" sheet**

2. **Click Page Layout tab.**

3. **On the Page Setup group, click the dialog launcher**

4. **On the Page Setup window, select the Page tab and select the Landscape option for Orientation.**

5. **In the Paper Size text box select B5 from the dropdown**

6. **Select the Margins tab and enter 0 in the Spin Button for the Buttom margin.**

7. **In the Centre on page section, select both the horizontal and vertical boxes and click OK.**

8. **Select the "Headers and Footers" sheet. While pressing the Ctlr Key, activate both the FormatMe1 and FormatMe2 sheets. This will select all three sheets as a group.**

9. **With the three sheets selected, click the Page Setup dialog launcher.**

10. **When the Page Setup window opens, close it again. This will transfer the settings for the source sheet ("Headers & Footers") to the other two sheets.**

11. **Right-click one of the three sheets and click "Ungroup Sheets" in the context menu.**

Ex4_Q17.

Provide the appropriate settings on the "**Chart**" sheet so that when the sheet is printed only the data will be printed. The chart should <u>not</u> be printed along with the data.

1. Right-click the <u>chart area</u> and select "**Format Chart Area**" from the context menu.

2. In the **Format Chart Area** dialog screen, click the "**Size & Properties**" icon

3. Click the arrow that points to "**Properties**" to expand it.

4. Uncheck the "**Print Object**" checkbox

Ex4_Q18.

Using the Custom Views worksheet as parent sheet, create a custom view with column C and column D hidden. Leave all other columns unhidden. Name the custom view "My Custom View".

1. **In the Custom View sheet, highlight columns C and D.**

2. **Right-click on the highlighted range and select "Hide" from the context menu.**

3. **Click View Workbook Views Custom Views.**

4. **On the Custom View screen, click the Add button.**

5. **In the Add View screen, enter "My Custom View" in the Name textbox.**

Ex4_Q19.

You work for a company called "**ThreePointEight Consulting**". Configure Excel options such that when you type "**3Pt8**" into a cell, the cell should display your company's name (i.e. "**ThreePointEight Consulting**")

1. **Select File → Options → Proofing**

2. **Click the "AutoCorrect Options…" button**

3. **In the "Replace:" textbox, type "3Pt8"**

4. **In the "With:" textbox, type "ThreePointEight Consulting"**

5. **Click OK**

Ex4_Q21.

Provide the required print options so that Excel will print the 2 comments on the "**Printing**" sheet at the end of the printout.

1. **Click Page Layout on the Ribbon.**

2. **Click the Page Setup dialog launcher**

3. **Select the Sheet tab**

4. **In the Comments dropdown,**

   select "At the end of sheet" and click OK

Ex4_Q22.

On the **Pivot Table** sheet, add a second instance of the **Location** field to the **Value** section. Change the name of that value to "**Pct**". Show each value of the **Pct** field as percent of the total of the (**Pct**) column.

1. Click a cell within the pivot table data so show the **Pivot Table Fields task pane**.

2. Drag the **Location** field to the **Value** section.

3. Click on the field (just added the **Value** section) and select "**Value Field Settings…**"

4. In the **Custom Name** box, type "**Pct**" and click **OK**

5. Right-click any cell under the **Pct** column and select **Show value As % of Column Total.**

Ex4_Q23.

"Ex4_Q23 is deliberately left blank"

Ex4_Q24.

On the Budget – Division 1 worksheet, paste the list of range names starting from cell I5.

1. Select cell I5

2. **In the Defined Names group, click "Use in Formula" dropdown**

3. Click **Paste Name**.

4. In the "**Paste Name**" dialog box, click the "**Paste List**" button

Notes:

_____

_____

_____

_____

_____

Ex4_Q25.

Apply the **General** format as the <u>default</u> format for the workbook.

Notes:

_____

_____

_____

_____

1.   Select the **Home** tab **Style Cell Style** drop-down.

2.   **Right-click the Normal Style → Modify..** Select the **General** format. Click **OK.**

Ex4_Q26.

On the **West Companies** sheet, modify the existing **Conditional Formatting** rule to remove the values from then **2015 Sales** column and show only the data bars.

Notes:

_____

_____

_____

_____

1. Click **Home** ➜ **Style** group ➜ **Conditional Formatting**. In the dropdown, select **Manage Rule**

2. On the **Show format rule for** drop-down box select "**This Worksheet**"

3. Activate the **Data Bar** rule and click **Edit Rule…**

4. Click the **Show bar only** text box

Ex4_Q27.

On the **Feb Humidity** sheet, highlight (using Red colour) all humidity values that are <u>**less**</u> than their corresponding **Jan Humidity** values.

Notes:

1. Select the humidity values on the **Feb Humidity** sheet (**B2:H21**).

2. Click the **Home** tab. In the **Style** group, click the **Conditional Formatting** drop-down

3. Select the **Manage Rules…** option

4. On the **Conditional Formatting Rules Manager** dialog box, click the **New Rule** tab.

5. Select the **Use a formula to determine which cells to format** option.

6. In the **Format values where this formula is true** text box, type the following formula: ' ='Jan Humidity'!B2>B2

7. Click the **Format** tab and in the **Colour** drop-down select **Red.**

Ex4_Q28.

In the **Auto Fill** sheet, Create an **Auto Fill** using the cities in cells **A3:A11**. Type **Sydney** in cell **C3** and drag the **Fill handler** to auto-fill cells **C4:C11** with the rest of the cities (just as in cells **A3:A11**).

Notes:

1. Click File ➜ **Options** ➜ **Advanced**

2. Scroll down and click the **Edit Custom List** button (in the General section).

3. In the **List Entries** list box, enter the cities (Sydney….Newcastle)", separated by commas

4. Click **Add** and then click **OK**

5. In the **Auto Fill** sheet, select cell **C3**, enter **Sydney**

6. Drag down to fill the cells

Ex4_Q29.

In the Status Chart worksheet, change the chart layout to Layout 1, change the chart title to Employment History and change the chart style to Style 9. Save the chart as a chart template to the PureSoftwareTemplate folder in your documents folder and with the name EmploymentChart

Notes:

1. Select the Status Chart worksheet. On this worksheet, select the chart

2. Click Chart Tools Design Chart Layouts group and click the Quick Layout dropdown, and select Layout 1

3. Click on Chart Title and type "Employment History"

4. In the Chart Tools Design tab, locate the Chart Styles group and click the drop down. Select Style 9

5. Right click the chart and click Save as Template. Navigate to the PureSoftwareTemplate folder in your documents folder, name the template EmploymentChart and click Save.

Ex4_Q30.

Using a named formula called "**Address**", the **INDEX** function and the **MATCH** function, provide a means to retrieve the address into cell **G3** for a name entered in cell **G1**. Use one of the names in the **A3:A10** range. Ensure that no error message is shown if the name does not exist in the list. If the name does not exist the address cell (**G3**) must be blank.

Notes:

1. Click **Formula Define Names Define Name**

2. In the **New Name** dialog box, enter "**Address**" into the **Name** textbox

3. In the "**Refers to:**" textbox, enter:

=IFERROR (INDEX($A$3:$B$10, MATCH($G$1,$A$3:$A$10,0),2),"") and click **OK**

INDEX

A

Access Databasse, 93, 94, 97, 98
AdventureWorks SSAS database, 125, 126
AdventureWorks SSAS.abf, 124

C

CALCULATE function, 114
calculated field, 57, 58, 59, 60, 61, 65, 66, 67, 68, 104, 115
calculated item, 57, 61, 63, 64, 67
Columns Area, 2
COLUMNS area, 8
Compact layout, 25
Conditional Formatting, 75, 77, 78, 79, 80

D

Data Connection Wizard, 96
Data Mining, 125
Data Model, 86, 87, 88, 89, 91, 92, 93, 97, 98, 99, 100, 101, 102, 103, 106, 107, 108, 109, 111, 113, 117
Data Source, 3, 4, 5, 7, 16, 17, 38, 92, 182
Data View, 108
DATE table, 111
DAX RELATED function, 110
Defer Layout Update, 17, 18
Diagram View, 104, 108
Dimension, 128, 129
Distinct Count, 103

E

External Data Source, 92, 102

F

Filter area, 10
Filtering in your pivot table, 45
Filters area, 2, 51, 67

G

Get External Data, 94, 96, 97, 105

H

Hierarchy, 128

I

Insert Slicer dialog, 12
Insert Slicers dialog, 53
Insert Timeline dialog, 15, 73

L

Label Filter fly-out, 50
Layout & Format tab, 23, 51
Levels, 128

M

Manage Relationships, 90, 91, 98
Management Studio (SSMS), 124
Measures, 129
Member, 129
multiple consolidation ranges, 81

N

Number Format, 21, 34

O

Office 365 Business, 99
Office Professional Plus, 99
OLAP cube, 125, 128, 129
OLAP databases, 125
Online Analytical Processing, 125
Outline Form layout, 26, 32
Outline Layout, 40

P

Pivot Charts can evolve, 75
pivot table report, 1, 3, 4, 5, 16, 19, 20, 26, 43, 45, 50, 52
PivotChart, 69, 72, 81, 136, 145, 162
PivotTable Field List, 8, 17, 18, 21, 102, 145, 162
PivotTable Fields list, 43, 59, 88, 95, 102, 103, 106, 128
PivotTable Fields List, 100, 101, 102, 109, 112
PivotTable Options, 23, 51
PivotTable Style gallery, 20, 21, 28
Power View, 116, 118, 119, 122, 123
PowerPivot add-in, 3, 99, 104
PowerPivot engine, 99

R

Recommended PivotTable, 11

RELATEDTABLE, 110

Report Connection, 14, 56

Report Connections, 13, 14

Report Filter Pages, 52, 53

REPORT LAYOUT

making changes, 24

Rows Area, 1

ROWS drop zone, 8

S

SharePoint Server, 104

Show Values As, 33, 34, 44, 183

Slicer Tools Options, 14

sort in ascending order, 44

SQL Server, 3, 86, 93, 95, 96, 124

subtotals

display, 9, 24, 26, 31, 32, 33, 65, 66, 78

Switch Visualization, 118, 119

T

Table Element, 29

Table Import Wizard, 105

Tabular layout, 27, 43

Tabular layouts, 3

Time Intelligence Functions, 111, 113

Timeline filter, 45, 55

Timeline slicer, 14, 15

Top 10 Filter, 49

U

Ungrouping Your Data, 40

V

Value Field Setting, 21, 34

Value Field Settings, 21, 33, 34, 103, 187

Values Area, 1

VALUES drop zone, 8

VLOOKUP, 65, 99, 116, 143, 160, 173, 179

W

What-If analysis, 129

Printed in the United States
By Bookmasters

The Pivot Table is without doubt the most powerful data processing tool ever introduced by Microsoft into the Excel product tool set, rivalled only by its younger sibling Power BI. The ability of pivot tables to transform large quantities of data into clear, concise summary report is incredible.

The power of pivot tables as data processing tool is only limited by user knowledge and imagination, and unthinkably, there are some Excel users who know next to nothing about pivot tables.

This book is written by a Microsoft Office Specialist Expert (MOSE), and a Mining Engineer with extensive experience in Excel. The Author's experience in various Microsoft data management tools such as SQL Server, MS Access and the MS Business Intelligence tools are brought to the fore in this book. By the time you reach the middle of the book, you should be able to increase your productivity with the skills you have learned. Every chapter of the book gives you the chance to practice what you have learned with step-by-step exercises.

At the end of the book you are given over two hundred Excel exercises and step-by-step instructions to perform the exercises.

We guarantee that any serious reader who goes through the book and performs the exercises within the chapters of the book and those exercises compiled at the end would be well on the way to becoming an Excel expert and a pivot table guru.

If you want to take your learning experience even further, we have provided over sixty questions and answers at our website. You can purchase and download these exercises and begin your learning experience at your own pace. Each exercise includes an extensive video explanation and a walk-through solution, as well as a chance to import your own data to work with.

SAM AKRASI is a Mining Engineer by profession and a data aficionado by nature. Sam has been involved in spreadsheet applications for over 30 years, beginning with the now-extinct products such as Symphony and Lotus 1-2-3. His training as a Mining Engineer and love for data have naturally led to his various assignment of processing large amounts of data in the resources industry and other similar industries.

Sam has earned a number of Microsoft certifications. Beginning in 1998, when he earned his first certification as a MS Access developer, Sam has maintained his interest in Microsoft data processing tools. He currently holds certifications in SQL Server, Microsoft Office (Excel) Specialist Expert (MOSE) and is currently on the last leg of his MCSE (Business Intelligence) certification. Sam is also a Microsoft Certified Trainer and currently doubles as a consultant and freelance trainer in Excel and the BI tools.

ISBN 978-1-5434-0588-0

Xlibris

9 781543 405880

WAYNE'S
WORLD
of PHYSICS

WRITTEN BY

CARREL W. UPTERGROVE